Praise for TRUST, INC.

"**Trust, Inc.** is filled with so many great thoughts, ideas, and tools that I think would be useful for a boss of any kind...or really anyone who works with other people."

—Paul W. King III, production manager, Specialty Food Merchandising

"**Trust, Inc.** is so much more than the title suggests! It will challenge your intellect, touch you emotionally, and open your eyes to how you can change yourself and those around you in a meaningful, powerful way. Reading Nan's book will undoubtedly propel you to a higher understanding of the why and the how of authentic work relationships. It is truly humbling and emotionally moving to find a piece of writing so electrifying in its wisdom."

—Peter Krajeski, HR manager, PA Leadership Charter School, Palcs.org

"**Trust, Inc.** helped me to identify the part I play in elevating trust to help cultivate a more creative and innovative project team. Nan's writing style, with real-world examples, immediately painted a picture of today with hope for tomorrow. This book is honest and engaging, and calls for insight to help cultivate trust in our teams. I have tangible action items that I can incorporate into my daily work life to build better software products with happier, more fulfilled team members."

—G. Young, senior project manager

Praise for the Author

"I would trust Nan Russell to drive 'My Bus' with myself and all of my team with me to anywhere in the world."

—Diane Hennessy, store manager, Macy's Leadership Award Winner

"I have followed Nan's writings for years and always look forward to her next article or book. Nan has a way of giving real-life, practical examples anyone can relate to and helps you come to your own insights by seeing an experience through her reflections."

—Eleanor Gathany, GPHR, senior regional HR leader, Amazon

"Nan Russell is a leader who feeds the passion in all who work with her. She has the ability to bring out the very best in everyone she comes in contact with."

—Gloria S. Baladez, manager HR operations and experience, QVC

TRUST, INC.

**How to Create a Business Culture That Will
Ignite Passion, Engagement, and Innovation**

TRUST, INC.

NAN S. RUSSELL

CAREER
PRESS

Pompton Plains, N.J.

TRUST, INC.
EDITED AND TYPESET BY KARA KUMPEL
Cover design by Rob Johnson/Toprotype
Printed in the U.S.A.

To order this title, please call toll-free 1-800-CAREER-1 (NJ and Canada: 201-848-0310) to order using VISA or MasterCard, or for further information on books from Career Press.

The Career Press, Inc.
220 West Parkway, Unit 12
Pompton Plains, NJ 07444
www.careerpress.com

Library of Congress Cataloging-in-Publication Data
Russell, Nan S.
  Trust, inc. : how to create a business culture that will ignite passion, engagement, and innovation / by Nan S. Russell.
      pages cm
  Includes bibliographical references and index.
    ISBN 978-1-60163-285-2 (pbk.) -- ISBN 978-1-60163-508-2 (ebook) 1. Leadership. 2. Trust. 3. Employee motivation. 4. Corporate culture. I. Title.

  HD57.7.R868 2013
  658.3'14--dc23
                                                                    2013036047

This book is dedicated to my parents, who taught me through their life's actions the meaning of authentic trust.

In memory of my father, C. Franklin Schindler, who believed everyone deserved a fair chance, your word is as binding as a contract, a job without passion is work, and you must bring your music to your world.

And to my mother, Nancy Friend Schindler, whose joyful, playful, and loving spirit saw, nurtured, and sought the best in people, and who still operates with a compassionate heart and the philosophy to give more than you get from life.

Acknowledgments

No one can whistle a symphony. It takes a whole orchestra to play it.
-H.E. Luccock

I wanted to write a book about trust for a *very* long time. Its tune played in and around my work for years. But bringing out a connected and integrated melody only occurred because a few people trusted my passion, believed in the message, and helped me shape its essence. I'm grateful to each of you who worked on this book—helping it come together, pushing to make it better, and ensuring its message gets heard. Although my name appears on the cover, yours is woven into its core.

I'm indebted to my wonderful agent, Lisa Hagan, of Lisa Hagan Literary, who believed in the book's idea and brought it to light with Career Press, enabling me to once again work with a terrific publisher. A special thanks to the entire Career Press team, including Ron Fry, Michael Pye, Adam Schwartz, Laurie Ann Kelly-Pye, Jeff Piasky, Gina Talucci, and Kirsten Dalley.

I'm indebted to my friend and colleague Beth Pelkofsky, who, even after 20 years working together, still says yes to new projects and brings her thoughtful perspective to multiple drafts, enhancing my words and augmenting my thinking. And to Jill Dodds, whose persistence and resourcefulness helps me stay writing while she checks facts, verifies statements, obtains permissions, and lets me stop worrying.

I'm indebted to bosses I've worked for and people I've worked with, who trusted me and by doing so created an environment that enabled my learning, growth, and contribution. I'm also indebted to the people who didn't trust, made work difficult, and demonstrated the tangible impact of distrust. You shaped the work I do today.

I'm indebted to family, friends, and readers who keep me grounded, encouraging, nudging, challenging, and supporting me. A very special thanks to my son Ian Russell, daughter-in-law Janine, and granddaughters Neva and Adelin who provide me not only joy, but tangible reasons to keep working for better work cultures for them and people everywhere.

Finally, I'm indebted to the one person who holds it all together for me—my best friend and husband of 38 years, Dan Russell, who edits my work, counters my thinking, and makes technology easy for me. But, that's not what he *really* does. He gets me, sees me, and creates a nurturing place with unconditional love that gives me the soul-courage to write.

With gratitude,
Nan S. Russell

CONTENTS

The *Why* Behind the Book

The best way to predict the future is to create it.
~Peter Drucker

I believe the seeds for this book began decades ago. Perhaps when I was 11 and my then-BFF broke my heart; or maybe later when a teacher's promise turned false in a 9th-grade awards ceremony; or maybe when a boss I admired asked me to lie for her; or when a failed marriage challenged my self-trust; or when money was confiscated by our builder; or...you get the point.

My broken-trust experiences are no different from yours. We all have them. We all know the pain, disappointment, and anger of giving our trust, only to have it betrayed. We all know how foolish we feel, how vulnerable and gullible, and "taken." And we all know we don't ever want to feel that way again. We also know how disheartening and unfulfilling it is to work with or for people you can't trust or who don't trust you. Yet, that's the reality for most.

The trust deficit isn't just in Washington, D.C.; it plagues most workplaces. At a time when our economy continues to struggle, employee engagement is down, job satisfaction is low, and trustworthiness is the most wanted quality in a boss, there's another reality: *The Great Recession impacted more than the economy.* Trust between employers and employees was broken.[1]

Let me be very clear about the book's message: The *why* behind writing this book *isn't broken trust.* That's not the message, purpose, or intention of what you'll find in these pages. I wrote this book because I'm passionate about, and committed to, creating a better future. This book is not about the problem of distrust, but the real-world, everyday, simple workplace solutions for creating, nurturing, and sustaining authentic trust in *your* work group, your *Trust: Inc.* This book is about new possibilities, not old problems.

Throughout the years, I've been interested in the topic of trust. I've spent time reading, researching, thinking, learning, and teaching about trust. And what I know is this: Trust matters. It brings out the best in us and reminds us who we are. It makes us, and those around us, better.

But here's what I also know about trust. As author Jack R. Gibb wrote, "Trust opens the doorways to the spirit." I know trust brings deep connections, new understandings, personal growth, and discovery. I know it ignites passions, creativity, and authenticity. And I know without it, there are no genuine relationships.

While not denying broken trust, workplace problems, or organizational hurdles, the book is about what *you* can affect *right now*; what you can do to create a better future for yourself and those you lead.

I wrote this book because I believe people like you can change the course at work. My personal goal is to know that my 4-year-old granddaughter, Adelin, and her 6-year-old sister, Neva, and those of their generation, will find waiting for them a Trust, Inc.—a culture enabling their talents, ideas, and possibilities. I believe the way to a better workplace, and a better world, is by doing what we can do together to affect that future. And it all begins with trust.

INTRODUCTION
Trust Is a Local Issue

Trust, not technology, is the issue of the decade.
~Tom Peters

Like a societal Doctor Jekyll and Mister Hyde, trust confounds us. On one hand we live in unparalleled times of global interdependence, instant connection, and no-worries access (at least in developed countries) to abundant and safe water, food, and medical care. Most of us don't think twice about swiping plastic cards at registers, answering e-mails from strangers, ordering items online, or flying across the country.

On the other hand, we live in a time when computer magic renders real photographs indistinguishable from enhanced ones, truth-in-advertising is an oxymoron, and reminders of the perils of trusting, such as seven-time Tour de France winner Lance Armstrong's doping admission or former mayor of New Orleans' corruption charges related to Katrina hurricane recovery, fill headlines.

A 24/7 news cycle, augmented by social media, ensures our access to trust-breaking stories about child-harming priests, lying and manipulation in politics, and misdeeds of business executives. Most weren't surprised when Pew Research reported, "Only 22 percent of the public trust government in Washington almost always or most of the time."[1] We were unfazed when Gallup found, "Americans' confidence in banks is at a historic low."[2] And we didn't blink when a Maritz poll informed us, "Only 10% of employees trust management to make the right decisions in times of uncertainty."[3] Yet, when teachers in Atlanta falsified standardized test scores by erasing wrong answers and supplying correct ones, one had to wonder, "*Who* can you trust?"

Trust is challenging. Part of our Jekyll-Hyde dichotomy about what and whom we trust is attributable to the word *trust* itself. People mean different things when they use the word, often interchangeably with words like reliable or predictable or trustworthy. It's a word fraught with multiple definitions, interpretations, and expectations. There are even different kinds of trust—confidence trust, competence trust, organizational trust, institutional trust, basic trust, authentic trust, blind trust, self-trust, situational trust, transactional trust, stakeholder trust, brand trust, leadership trust, and more.

This book is about *authentic trust*. It's the trust that's broken or missing in most workplaces. It's the trust, when present, that fuels innovation and engagement, and ignites passions in those we lead. And it's the trust you'll need for *your* Trust, Inc. Here's a glimpse:

authentic trust \ *verb*. \ 1. Trust(ing), as in committing to, giving, or placing confidence in another, with awareness and optimism. **2.** Choosing actions associated with genuine relationship-creating, -building, -restoring; requires ongoing cultivation. **3.** A dynamic happening *in* relationships, created and grown only when there is an ongoing commitment to the relationship, and when that relationship is more important than any single outcome. Accepts risk of trust-betrayed. **4.** Given without concern for personal advantage, enabling others to show up with talents and do great work. **5.** Requires self-awareness; a relationship practice with one's self that offers ways to explore individual gifts, possibilities, and potential.

THERE'S A PROBLEM AT WORK

You don't need an expert to confirm what you already know and Gallup polling continues to substantiate: The majority of employees are disengaged at work. You don't need an employee survey to tell you why discretionary efforts are tamed, passions for work are fleeting, and ideas are tethered. And you don't need a consultant to explain why cynicism is up, enthusiasm is down, and trust is the currency of the new workplace. All you need to do is reread one of Aesop's fables, "The Goose that Laid the Golden Egg." Remember the greedy farmer who wanted more than one golden egg each day? By the story's end, he'd killed the goose and was left with no golden eggs at all.

Every day, leaders at all levels communicate with their actions that they're not committed to a working relationship with those they lead. They eliminate resources and positions while still expecting immediate results. They shut out dialogue and limit open communication, while still requesting candid feedback. They pocket stock options and bonuses, while reducing staff salary and benefits. They reward unfavorable behaviors, while operating with myopic interests and escalating bureaucracy. And then they wonder why those they're striving to engage are alienated, distrustful, and fed-up.

You don't need an expert to explain that while basic productivity and job presence can be bought, staff ideas and discretionary efforts must be freely given. When intellectual property (the golden egg) is the competitive edge for *most* enterprises, success is contingent upon natural followership and significant relationships built through authentic trust. A 20th-century mindset that sees employees as interchangeable pieces won't fuel innovative products and services or enhance customer impressions in this 21st century.

You don't need an expert to tell you that out-of-touch leaders, operating like medieval warlords with refrains like "just make it happen," "there's no budget," "I don't care what it takes," and "they should be thankful they have a job" have fueled employee mindsets, exacerbating the challenges we collectively face. Employees know what many leaders haven't figured out: Parental, top-down cultures in today's world are as ineffective as one-size-fits all, print-only marketing approaches.

IT'S A SHARED PROBLEM

It's time we were also honest about the challenge. Trust is not only about "them," in corporate, political, or business roles; it's also about *us*, in everyday roles. What's needed to change our direction is a balanced understanding. Consider these representative examples:

- In a CareerBuilder.com survey, employers reported nearly "half of the resumes contained falsehoods."[4]

- Data-mining experts from the University of Illinois estimate "one-third of all consumer reviews on the Internet are fake."[5]

- The largest for-profit hospital with 163 U.S. facilities discovered cardiologists were "unable to justify many of the procedures they were performing."[6]

- In a magazine survey, 63 percent of employees admitted to calling out sick when they weren't.[7]

- Almost 50 percent of a Harvard University class was investigated for suspected cheating, on a take-home final exam, in what the undergraduate dean called "unprecedented in its scope and magnitude."[8]

Reduced trust impacts relationships, bottom lines, innovative solutions, cooperative endeavors, and well-being. Trust is a collective problem when it impacts the society we share; when the *win* becomes more important than *how* it's achieved.

THERE'S A LOCAL SOLUTION

Most of us aren't going to rebuild organizational trust, increase confidence in CEOs, or change perceptions of corner-office leaders. We aren't going to change our boss's behavior, or that of bosses above her, or be tapped to awaken those who cling to 20th-century workplace myths, or operate with misconceptions of what works at work today. But that shouldn't stop those who lead from replenishing the trust deficits in their business, work group, or relationships.

In this era of distrust, disengagement, and disconnection, if you want a thriving business or career, you can't afford to allow what you *can't* change to affect what you *can*. If you're someone's immediate boss, no matter your organizational level or business role, you can positively influence trust, commitment, engagement, and innovation. You can create your Trust, Inc.—a trust-pocket, where people show up and do great work.

There are three reasons trust is a local solution for work groups everywhere:

1. People Work for People

Trust isn't about "those" people in senior management; it's about us in our individual work groups. If someone works for you, it's *your* trust that matters most to them. You're the one having everyday impact on their work life.

Can they trust you? Can they count on you? Are you worthy of their trust? Do you trust them? These issues affect both their results and yours. Don't be naïve in thinking trust is only about others. For the people who work for you, it's about you.

2. No Permission Is Needed

Which business, team, department, or work group gets the best results where you work? You'll find trust there. Where do you notice energetic people, unleashed creativity, and unstoppable enthusiasm? There's trust there. Where are people giving more than what's asked, volunteering for assignments, and accomplishing the unexpected? Trust is at work there too.

Anyone, anywhere can start his or her Trust, Inc. You don't need permission to build great working relationships, exceed expectations, enjoy the results of staff engagement, or lead an enthusiastic team. You don't need to wait for your boss to give you trust, or for an organizational trust-building initiative to launch. Authentic trust is something you make. It's an action. You choose; you decide.

There's even a nudge from the Conference Board's CEO Challenge study, which for the first time included "trust in business" in the top-10 challenges "after several chief executives warned that lack of trust could pose a serious threat to growth."[9]

3. People Trust "a Person Like Me"

As societal distrust in established institutions, politicians, and business leaders grows, "a person like me" is one of the most credible sources to which people listen.[10] As people seek trusted information, not from their institutions or organizational leaders, they're moving from institutional trust toward individual trust.

That shift changes the influencers. It makes what you do and how you do it even more important. With the shift toward individual trust, you're a catalyst for rebuilding the trust deficit plaguing workplaces and communities. For those who report to you, you're a person "like them." Trust at work is a local relationship issue. It's invested and built person to person. Building trust locally means positively influencing your environment.

Imagine millions and millions of trust-pockets thriving across hundreds of thousands of organizations and businesses, operated by people just like you. When I hold that picture, I'm reminded of words from tennis legend Arthur Ashe: "To achieve greatness: start where you are, use what you have, do what you can."

People work for people, not for companies. Even in an era when "skeptical" has turned to "cynical" about everyone from politicians to priests, doctors to teachers, and CEOs to department heads, any supervisor, manager, or business owner can still build a trusting environment for their work group, where people can show up and do great work.

If you're someone's immediate supervisor, you can positively influence trust, engagement, and innovation. You don't need to wait for HR or top management to launch an initiative to rebuild trust, reignite passions, or reboot the work culture. Top-down programs aren't the answer to distrust and disengagement, *you are*.

Troubling trends and heart-grabbing headlines can reinforce the impression that no one is worthy of your trust. But they are.

WE NEED A NEW CURRENCY: TRUST

What companies need to ensure growth, innovation, and sustainability can't be bought with just a paycheck. Intellectual property and staff initiative are essential to organizational and societal success, but they require a different kind of currency: *trust*.

We're approaching an era when the strongest performers, those with the golden eggs of ideas, know-how, solutions, and innovation, will accept nothing less than work environments and bosses that enable them to do their best work. For those who want great results in this post-recession era, *the ability to build authentic trust is a new workplace essential.*

Authentic trust is the currency of winning cultures fueling the next generation of exceptional results. No one will need an expert to explain why those who can create, grow, and invest trust currency will thrive.

WHAT YOU'LL FIND IN THESE PAGES

This is a hands-on book for anyone with a staff. It's about how to create your Trust, Inc.—a local work-group culture that works, founded on authentic trust. It's not a book about trust per se, in a traditional way, nor a book about work-cultures, per se, in a typical way. Rather, it tackles the active, real-work process of using "trust" as an action to build your trust-pocket and get great results from yourself and others.

In **Part I** you'll find specifics about trust-pockets and trusted bosses, plus what it looks like to be making trust currency, and the dividends to expect from your trust investment—engagement, innovation, and accountability.

In **Part II**, expect specifics about what you'll need to do as a Trust, Inc. leader to make, build, and sustain trust.

Finally, **Part III** looks beyond Trust, Inc. to the setbacks and stumbling blocks you may encounter, including how to restore broken trust.

In every section, you'll find a "what does it look like" approach. My desire is to help you see what thriving work relationships founded on authentic trust look like, and how to create, nurture, grow, and wisely invest in them. You'll find approaches to help you apply these trust-making concepts in the real work world. Tips, examples, anecdotes, and how-tos are included, along with reflective exercises so you can garner your own insights and applicability.

What keeps you awake at night? What worries or frustrates you at work, or takes you away from what you do best, but requires your attention as a leader? The typical answer is: people. It's the people we lead, and work for and around, that complicate our work. And yet, these people also help us soar. Great work relationships, founded on trust, enable great results. But, to get those great work dividends means commitment, self-awareness, and continuous involvement on your part. Think of yourself as a trust-catalyst.

What you'll find in this book is good news, not just about what you can do in your work group, but also the potential beyond those imaginary boundaries. In today's work world, change can start from anywhere. The concept of achieving change by collective voices is taking shape. From changing bank fees to changing policies, people are using collective voices to amplify messages, unite with others, and impact direction. Your Trust, Inc. adds *your* voice.

Whereas trust is a very big topic, this book is narrowly focused on your trust, work group, impact, and career. There's much written on the topic of trust. Certainly, there are many ways to build trust, create winning results, and enhance trust-building skills. Plus, there are differences in style and approaches that speak to the uniqueness we bring to our work. So, I encourage you to take what works for you and leave the rest. But before you do, I hope you'll approach *Trust, Inc.* with openness and trust. It's from that space that these words were written, peppered with hope and optimism, about a local path to a better work future.

PART I

AT TRUST, INC., YOU DON'T NEED PERMISSION TO...

You cannot get through a single day without having an impact on the world around you. What you do makes a difference, and you have to decide what kind of difference you want to make.

~ Jane Goodall

CHAPTER 1

Create Your Trust-Pocket

If your actions inspire others to dream more, learn more, do more, and become more, you are a leader.

~ John Quincy Adams

Ebenezer Scrooge is not a typical model for leaders, but he's a good place to start. Working in his establishment would be the antithesis of a thriving, winning trust-pocket. Still, as self-serving and stone-hearted as Dickens's character appears, he did get a few things right. Scrooge didn't profess that Bob Cratchit was his most important asset, or suggest that if Bob worked harder he'd be rewarded. He didn't claim they were in it together, or that they were both suffering in economic downtimes. Ebenezer Scrooge rendered no unkept promises, offered no dangling carrots, and established no expectations that if deadlines were met, quarterly goals were achieved, or problems were solved, Bob would be rewarded, help would arrive, work-family balance would be restored, or working conditions would improve.

Of course, I'm not suggesting Scrooge's despicable management style is to be emulated, but our own nightmares await if work trust is not rebuilt. And for those who lead groups, manage teams, or run businesses, there are three insights worth learning from Ebenezer:

1. **What Scrooge said and did were in alignment.** What plagues work cultures 150 years after Scrooge's time is our misalignment. What bosses say and what they do are frequently disconnected, fueling distrust, disengagement, and discontent. Most bosses don't pause long enough to consider their actions through staff lenses, or perceive the unintended consequences occurring when their words and actions differ. But they need to.

2. **Scrooge was who he professed to be.** No insincere caring. No hollow praise. No hypocrisy. Bob Cratchit understood Scrooge's management style completely. Today, people still want bosses to be who they profess they are and show up consistently. How else can they judge their boss as good-hearted or manipulating, friend or foe, enabler or scammer? Of course, in this Knowledge Age, the work itself has changed, and people don't offer today's golden eggs to Scrooge-like bosses.

3. **Scrooge accepted feedback, made self-adjustments, and changed.** The transformation of Ebenezer Scrooge from self-serving boss to enlightened man is more harrowing than most workplace "Aha!" moments. And it's more instant than building authentic trust. But openness to transforming our ways is as powerful today as it was then. And operating with trust currency is transformational for people and results.

If you choose to create your own Trust, Inc. (your thriving trust-pocket) you'll discover, as did Scrooge, that new ways bring brighter days—in your case, a path of positive impact, with rewards that include genuine relationships, personal growth, and exceptional results, as well as more opportunities, low attrition, and higher well-being.

This chapter offers the basics. Consider it the equivalent of Scrooge's visitations by the ghosts of the past, present, and future: By the end, he knew what he wanted to do; hopefully, you will too. Here's your first glimpse of your future:

> **Trust, Inc.** \ *noun*. \ **1.** A thriving pocket of trust (a.k.a. trust-pocket) where passion, engagement, innovation, and great work flourishes. **2.** A place where trust currency is made. **3.** A work group, requiring no formal approval or permission, that enables authentic trust. **4.** A self-created winning culture led by a trusted boss. **5.** A business culture operating with sustainable trust currency that regularly pays dividends.

OPERATE WITH *TRUST* AS A VERB

There are two kinds of people at work: those who function with trust only as a noun (a belief, condition, or state), and those who operate with trust as a verb (the action of making or giving) *and* a noun (a medium of relationship exchange). Noun people tend to make decisions similar to one of Marissa Mayer's, CEO of Yahoo: She decided to eliminate "elsewhere" work, requiring everyone to work in the office, giving the perception that Yahoo employees can't be trusted. To noun people trust means the "reliance on another party (i.e. person, group, or organization) under a condition of risk."[1] So in times of risk, they use strategies in which control trumps trust.

Those who get great results in the new workplace operate with trust as a verb. They understand that trust begets trust. Behavioral scientists at the University of Zurich have confirmed experimentally that "if you trust people, you make them more trustworthy." And, conversely, "sanctions designed to deter people from cheating actually make them cheat."[2] Whether people work in the office or somewhere else, there are always a few who will exploit the system, but noun people fail to realize that withholding trust reduces the exact behaviors they want and need.

Those who build trust-pockets are verb people. As authors Robert Solomon and Fernando Flores crystallize in their book, *Building Trust in Business, Politics, Relationships, and Life*, "Trust isn't something we have, or a medium or an atmosphere within which we operate. Trust is something we do, something we make."[3]

Authentic trust (defined in the Introduction) is essential to trust-pockets. Authentic trust is about the relationship and what it takes to create, build, and maintain mutually beneficial working relationships. Authentic trust isn't a belief about reliability or dependability, nor glue that "makes things possible." Rather, it's an active process of relationship building. People who want to enable engagement, innovation, creativity, and great work give authentic trust.

The Making of Trust Currency

You can pay for someone's time at work, and people will show up and do what they need to do. But you can't suction ideas, discretionary efforts, and innovative solutions from their minds. That's where trust currency comes in. It creates the medium of exchange in your trust-pocket.

As a Trust, Inc. leader you need people's "golden eggs" freely given. Your staff wants things from you too, such as flexibility, meaningful work, personal development, and a culture in which they can show up and do great work. When you make trust currency by giving authentic trust, you render possible what you want and what they want, creating a culture of reciprocity and mutual support. That winning culture is fueled by the exchange of trust, a.k.a. trust currency.

trust currency \ *noun*. \ **1.** Generated by authentic trust; requires ongoing production. **2.** Creates the medium of exchange in workplaces for competitive necessities leaders can't buy with just a paycheck; e.g. intellectual property, discretionary efforts, ideas, innovation, engagement, accountability, commitment. **3.** Creates medium of exchange for staff-desired outcomes; e.g. flexibility, creativity, meaningful work, well-being, contribution, learning and personal development, self-motivation. **4.** Fuels winning cultures; increases reciprocity and mutual support. **5.** Provides tangible and intangible results and relationship dividends.

How to make authentic trust, and its resulting trust currency, is the topic of Chapter 6. But, bottom line—you're the catalyst. As the leader of Trust, Inc., you start the process. Trust starts because you give it. Trust currency is generated as you continue to incrementally give authentic trust, in exchange for things given back to you. It's not a blank check or an on-off switch, but it is created by specific actions, behaviors, and mutual accountability. Think of investing authentic trust in others and getting dividends in return. Here's how it works:

REFLECTIVE EXERCISE
You Can See Trust

To start your thinking about behaviors that impact the making of trust currency, consider the 10 behaviors below. Check those that are part of your regular operating style.

- ❑ You influence more by your actions than your words. You operate as the message, not the messenger, with an alignment between your words and actions.

- ❑ You're self-aware. You recognize the impact of your beliefs and actions on others, and are tuned in to others' needs, strengths, and perspectives.

- ❑ You give trust first. You realize trust evolves incrementally over time, and the way to start or rebuild trust is to give it in evolving stages.

- ❑ You use trust-elevating communication techniques. You own your message, actions, and mistakes, and authentically show up in the process.

- ❑ You bring the best of who you are to your work. You operate from a "best of self" core with characteristics like kindness, compassion, love, tolerance, and integrity.

- ❑ You want the best for others. You aren't playing a game in which only one or two people win and the rest don't. You help make the pie bigger for everyone.

❏ You tell considered stories. You understand that the stories you tell at work are impactful and you choose stories that positively influence the culture and those in it.

❏ You operate with dependable politics. You get things done the right way, with ethics, integrity, and positive intention that builds relationships.

❏ You collaborate, cooperate, consider, and contribute. You value relationships and build lasting ones not only by what you do, but also by how you do it.

❏ You demonstrate competence as your starting point. You do what you say you can and will do, you do it well, and you assist others along the way.

Self-scoring: Consider this your Scrooge-equivalent of glimpsing your present. If you checked 8 or more, you can feel confident you're using behaviors that will help you with the creation of trust currency. If 7 or less, you'll find plenty of tips and how-tos in future chapters to increase your probability of producing the trust currency you need.

The bottom line is this: People don't give their ideas, discretionary efforts, enthusiasm, or best work to people they don't trust. Be the person they give their trust to and you'll harness trust-power in your work group—power to enlist the energy, talents, and gifts of individuals, to build teams, and to achieve amazing results.

WINNING TRUMPS *WIN*

There are two dominant work cultures in organizations: winning cultures and win cultures. Winning cultures operate with trust currency. They're founded on authentic trust, and fueled by five essentials for sparking and building trust (detailed in Part II). Winning cultures are work environments where passionate people share their talents, collaborate on ideas, go above and beyond, assist the greater whole, and do great work. They're high-performing and high-energy cultures, where people are engaged contributors. A winning culture is what Trust, Inc. leaders work to create.

> **winning culture** \ *noun*. \ **1.** A place, founded on authentic trust, where people can offer the best of who they are. **2.** An environment that fosters and enables trusting relationships, collaboration, teamwork, engagement, integrity, ethics, authenticity, innovation, communication, and great work. **3.** A work climate operating with winning at working approaches, a winning philosophy, and organizational values.

By contrast, win cultures lack authentic trust or withhold trust. Fueled by top-down, leader-dictated approaches, getting things done can be slowed by bureaucracy, silos, rules, regulations, and dark-side company politics.

Often highly competitive, with only a few who "win" or hold power, win cultures place premiums on outcome only, sometimes leaving the impression that "how it's done" circumvents common sense or ethics. There's secrecy and closed-door decision-making. Those who work in these cultures find rumors rampant, misinformation common, and trust-based relationships rare.

In a <u>win</u> culture, people are...	In a <u>winning</u> culture, people are...
Failing to respond; ignoring e-mails	Honoring commitments
Operating outside the norm	Operating with integrity and ethics
Using intimidation and manipulation	Showing kindness and consideration
Hoarding ideas; withholding information	Sharing ideas and information
Opposing or blocking others' progress	Helping others succeed
Doing only what's asked	Bringing their best; delivering more
Operating as if one size fits 95%	Making it personal; seeing each other
Blaming and finger-pointing	Operating with personal accountability
Showing fear and frustration	Bringing inspiration and hope
Retiring on the job	Using strengths and talents
Getting results through power and rank, carrots and sticks	Getting results through cooperation, teamwork, engagement, and trust

There are many misconceptions about work cultures. They're not all-or-none, top-down-only, or static. You can work in a company with an overall "win" culture and still manage and operate your group with a "winning" one (see Chapter 11). It can be a little harder that way; I've been there. But your staff will notice. And what you achieve together will be noticed too, with others wanting to figure out what you're doing differently and to emulate your success. I've seen profound organizational shifts started by trust-pockets persistently delivering exceptional results. It's hard to argue with great results created in the right way. In today's workplace, change doesn't have to start at the top. It can start from anywhere.

YOUR WINNING CULTURE— YOUR TRUST, INC.

For more than 25 years, the Great Place to Work® Institute has studied winning work cultures and the power of trust. Their findings conclude: "Trust is the single most important ingredient in making a workplace great."[4] If you want to make your work environment great for those you lead, start a trust-pocket. If you want to work in a winning culture yourself, start a trust-pocket. And if you want to achieve great results, start a trust-pocket. Authentic trust doesn't automatically find its way into everyday interactions, or stay like a screensaver in the background until it's needed. It's a decision, an action, a choice about the kind of leader you want to be.

The following 10 basics are intended as a philosophical framework of what's required to start, grow, and enhance a Trust, Inc. culture. These trust-pocket building blocks are applicable to any leader, at any level, in any role. If you're interested in creating and nurturing a winning culture, consider these the touchstones you'll need along the way. They're the ones to come back to when personal or organizational pressures push you off course.

1. Step Up

Stepping up involves an inner rather than outer behavior. Winning cultures founded on trust don't start and evolve by proclamation; they're created by desire, nurtured by authenticity, and evolved by behavioral integrity. Love doesn't thrive merely because you're in a committed relationship; neither does trust. Effectively handling setbacks, enabling ongoing communication, nurturing each others' strengths, dealing with differences, and making a continuous commitment to the relationship allow trust (and love) to flourish.

The process of stepping up involves self-assessment. First, do you have what it takes to lead a trust-pocket? Second, do you want to? People can learn to lead with trust, nurture a winning culture, and create a Trust, Inc. where people can shine and bring exceptional results. But few do. What about you?

2. Start With Competence—Yours!

Knowing you have the ability to deliver what you say, and that you will, is a starting point for trust. If people don't view you as competent, there's no performance trust. Without performance trust, you're unlikely to engage others, build lasting relationships, or demonstrate results. That's key in any winning culture. People trust people who consistently deliver.

Even if you give authentic trust, for trust currency to be produced and evolve, competence must be present. We all know the person everyone enjoys being around, but when it comes to asking her to be part of a critical project, or trusting her to make it happen—in other words, "choosing to risk making something you value vulnerable to another person's actions,"[5] we don't. Competence drives this element of trust.

3. Build on What's Going Right

A common trust-building mistake is spending energy to fix what's wrong, or focusing on those who are causing problems. Instead, identify and reinforce what's going right. Put your attention on getting more of the behaviors and actions you desire. Remember, whatever gets rewarded gets done. So, if you find Whitney's "5 Daily Snippets" a quick way to be alerted to issues in her area, tell her, and suggest she broaden distribution. Then encourage others to do something similar.

When you reinforce what's going well, you get more of it. Focus on the negative, and you often get more of that because attention can be its own reward. Help people see what it looks like to be successful in your work group, and you build trust. Plus, their actions will start aligning with that picture.

4. Be Bigger Than You

Trust-pockets don't thrive on supporting a boss's quarterly goals or meeting department or sales objectives. These will happen as by-products, but aren't what taps people's passions. Are you excited to go to work to help your boss get a bonus, or increase shareholder value? Most people aren't.

People need a reason that goes beyond tasks—a purpose. Some call it vision or mission. It doesn't matter the label, just be sure it's there. What's the purpose behind your team's tasks? Not the little purpose—the big purpose. Every person in your group needs to know why what they do matters to the whole.

Let's say your department is responsible for posting and process-ing patient payments. These are tasks. The tasks' purpose might fund your organization's healthcare professionals to save community lives. Saving lives matters. Help people get beyond their tasks, and they will; help them see their work matters, and it will.

5. Bring out the Best in Others

There's one sure way to bring out the best in others: Bring out the best in yourself. When you bring your best you to your work, you raise the bar for others to do the same. But it goes beyond that. When you help others use their strengths and talents at work, engagement happens. Gallup found that when leaders fail to focus on individual strengths, the odds of an employee being engaged "are just 9 percent." But when they do, the "odds soar to almost 73 percent."[6]

Engaging others' strengths means knowing what their strengths are and finding or creating ways they can use them. American philosopher Elbert Hubbard said, "It is a fine thing to have ability, but the ability to discover ability in others is the true test." That may be as simple as allowing people discretionary time to embrace a favorite project, or as complex as shifting responsibilities so people can use their talent. People trust people who bring out the best in them.

6. Make It Easier for Them

Those who operate trust-pockets don't see their job as managing others. Instead, they enable them, helping them succeed. They view their role as managing tasks, goals, and processes—not people—and pride themselves on their ability to clear roadblocks, enhance clarity, maneuver potholes, procure resources, and eliminate time-wasters.

Better, faster, easier, fun. That's what it's like to work for these people. They're not satisfied doing what's always been done, and instead challenge the status quo to improve it. They're constantly learning and sharing, helping others to learn and grow too. They help others get results in easier ways. People who make it easier, not harder, to get work done build trust, loyalty, and reciprocal action.

7. Acquire Big-Team Players

Many people play on a team of one. But winning cultures require a big-team mindset, understanding that actions by one affect another. We're connected. What one department, company, or country does affects another department, company, or country. Winning cultures need big-team players.

There are two things to understand about these players. First, not everyone on your team should be on your team. Sometimes there's a mismatch of mindsets, personalities, talents, or objectives. Help people who won't thrive working for you find success elsewhere. Second, don't delegate team selection. You're the only person who knows what it takes to work with you, to work in your Trust, Inc., and to be successful on your team.

Most people select individuals at or below their own level of performance. The way you can build a winning culture for the long term is to continually raise the selection bar. Hire people who are smarter than, better than, or different from you. Promote or hire those who already operate with a big-team mindset, who already give authentic trust, demonstrate behavioral integrity, communicate effectively, apply dependable politics, and get results with or without being in charge. Big-team players see beyond the little work group, helping the bigger whole succeed. If your team operates that way, it influences trust-building well beyond your Trust, Inc.

8. Be Open to Curiosity

Staying in a state of curiosity enhances your trust-pocket. When you ask questions from openness and inquisitiveness, others feel heard. When you respond to ideas, suggestions, and input with inquiring non-judgment, you'll spark creativity and keep learning.

Being open to curiosity requires a mindful presence, which, according to mindfulness coach Sunada Takagi, means "we must lose our rightness of our position." She continues in her blog this way: "Mindfulness has to begin with a respect for the other person's dignity and rationality. By this I mean, no matter how much I might disagree with what they're doing, I make an effort to understand why they're doing it and what circumstances got them there. It means suspending my own views and really appreciating the situation completely from their perspective—not just intellectually, but in my heart."[7]

A connection develops when you're sincerely interested and curious about another's point of view, and mindful presence also enhances your ability to understand perspectives beyond your own. This approach enables seeds of a winning culture to sprout with trust.

9. Add Realism

Reality is a necessary component of thriving trust-pockets. Leaders of these cultures add realism to the mix. First, they understand that people make mistakes. Embracing this concept is essential for boss credibility and trust-success. How you respond to others' failures and mistakes, as well as your own, is a yardstick for building or diminishing your trust currency.

The second reality is that trust comes with risk. You'll make errors in trusting—I know I have. I've over-trusted and under-trusted; I've lost and gained relationships, money, and opportunities by trusting or distrusting. What I've learned the hard way was captured by 19th-century Italian Prime Minister Camillo di Cavour: "The man who trusts other men will make fewer mistakes than he who distrusts them."

10. Apply the Five Essentials

You help or hinder the reality of your Trust, Inc. by the uncommon behavior of doing. Take a peek at the five essentials to spark and build trust in a skeptical world, which comprise Part II of this book:

1. **Go first.**
2. **Elevate your communication.**
3. **Demonstrate behavioral integrity.**
4. **Show up authentically.**
5. **Build genuine relationships.**

You will also learn how to rebuild trust, handle setbacks, maneuver potholes, and respond to push-back.

Of course, knowing something and doing that thing are different matters. For example, I know if I eat fewer calories than I expend, I'll lose weight, but my doing is not always aligned with my knowing. The same goes for trust-pocket building. When you finish this book, you'll know how to ignite the passions, engagement, and innovation of those you lead, and how to create, nurture, build, and rebuild authentic trust. You'll know how to create a trusting environment where you and those you work with can thrive. But unless you do it, the trust currency needed for your career and business success remains locked in your head, not actively thriving in your Trust, Inc.

THE FUTURE YOU SEE

What it takes to build trust today is different from what it took even three years ago. The new workplace requires a new currency: trust. How much trust currency are you making? The following exercise asks you to consider what's occurring in your work group right now. Should you keep it that way or change it? Consider this your Scrooge equivalent of glimpsing your future.

REFLECTIVE EXERCISE
Keep It or Change It?

If 90% of the time you're happy with the way your work group is operating, circle **K** *for keep it; if you'd like to see the relationships or dynamics improve, circle* **C** *for change it.*

1. People keep me informed and updated; there are few surprises. K / C

2. My staff is great about meeting deadlines and keeping their commitments. K / C

3. People like each other, showing care and concern to one another. K / C

4. I'm proud of the results we achieve as a group; ideas flow freely. K / C

5. My boss is complimentary about the work the team does. K / C

6. Differences are resolved easily with healthy conflict. K / C

7. People volunteer for additional assignments and put in extra effort. K / C

8. One thing I don't have to be concerned about is staff accountability. K / C

9. People freely admit mistakes and errors, and quickly correct them. K / C

10. The group works well with other departments and leaders. K / C

11. People speak up or offer feedback; there's real discussion. K / C

12. Collaboration, cooperation, and contribution are department traits. K / C

13. I get few, if any, complaints from people about their coworkers. K / C

14. People operate with integrity and ethics; I can trust them. K / C

15. The group has big-team thinking, supporting others in the organization. K / C

16. Rumors, negative storytelling, and finger-pointing are infrequent. K / C

17. Relationships are built on openness and trust around here. K / C

18. There is little, if any turnover; people are engaged with their work. K / C

19. I know people will get behind big projects; they're energized by them. K / C

20. Meetings with staff are full of suggestions, input, and dialogue. K / C

Self-Scoring: Count the number of Ks. A score of 15 or above reflects, more often than not, behaviors and actions associated with trust currency—keep it.

Count the number of Cs. If there are more Cs than Ks, take note of the dynamics or behaviors in your work group you'd like improved or to happen more often. These are clues where trust is limited. Through time, you may wish to revisit this exercise and note changes.

REFLECTIVE THINKING
Looking Ahead

Consider these questions. Insights are more likely if you write your answers.

1. If I had the ability to start from scratch, which of the members of my current work group would I invite along? What is it about them that causes me to select them?

2. What worries me most about the challenges I face at work?

3. By this time next year, what issues would I like to see improved in my work group?

A CLOSING THOUGHT

I believe the best workplaces are yet to come, and the people who will replenish the trust-deficit we're facing and fuel a thriving economy are people like you. Founded on authentic trust, I believe you, and people like you, will create innovative work groups, pockets of trust, where talented people make a difference through their work, conquer 21st-century problems, and turn their optimistic energy into a better future. And I believe, like scholar John Schaar, "The future is not some place we're going, but one we're creating. The paths are not to be found, but made." Like Ebenezer Scrooge, you can chart a path toward a new future—the one *you* want.

CHAPTER 2
Engage the Disengaged

Hold yourself responsible for a higher standard than anyone else expects of you.

~ Henry Ward Beecher

I woke at 4 a.m. for a final practice before delivering a morning keynote at a conference, but my normal speaking preparations, including a mindset routine, changed abruptly when I found myself showering in darkness as three lights simultaneously went out. It wasn't just dark, it was pitch black. Not even a sliver of light seeped under the door from the bedroom where my husband slept soundly.

In the blackness, I wasn't sure how to climb out of the shower/bath combination to avoid hazards. I couldn't remember the bathroom layout. We'd arrived late the previous night and I hadn't paid attention to yet another hotel room. I'd executed my movements like a robot carrying out a program: mechanical on-the-road routines the night before and a sleepy entrance at 4 a.m. left me unable to navigate in the pitch-black bathroom. I could say life is like that too, and discuss the merits of staying in the moment...or comment that life sometimes leaves us wet and in the dark, grasping for light to find our way—but those thoughts are too philosophical for pitch-black mornings.

These are the times when your child throws up on the new outfit you picked specially for a meeting that isn't happening now that you're staying home; or when the dog runs away as you're leaving for an appointment, making you rudely late; when the dishwasher overflows on the new carpet. We know these mornings. They render us scrambling.

I was definitely scrambling when I arrived at the event. The time it took to wake my husband for help, get hotel maintenance to fix the electrical problem, and finish getting ready put me in a harried and less than positive state. But as I took the stage and looked at the audience, it hit me: This wasn't my morning. The audience didn't care if I'd had one of those mornings. They didn't care why I was out of sorts. They didn't care that my hair wasn't styled perfectly or my jacket needed more pressing. They didn't care because their morning wasn't about me; it was about them. It was their kick-off, their event, their day.

That "aha!" shifted my pitch-black morning into a brighter one. A day isn't mine, it's ours. We share it. How we show up and bring awareness and energy to others, even in passing, matters. In the words of author Annie Dillard, "How we spend our days is, of course, how we spend our lives." And how we impact others' days is, of course, how we impact our own.

It's from this vantage point the topic of engagement begins. How you show up at work affects how others do. Engaging others starts with engaging oneself. Then its power multiplies. Engaging passions, talents, and discretionary efforts sparks innovation, creativity, and results.

With 70 percent of employees "not engaged" or "actively disengaged" at work,[1] engagement is an elusive "golden egg" for most leaders. Yet, those operating with trust find different results. This chapter offers tips and insights to help you create a winning trust culture that enables engagement and ignites results.

WHAT DOES IT MEAN TO BE ENGAGED AT WORK?

The "same word, different definition" challenge plagues engagement just as it does trust. Some claim engagement is "a rebrand of something that's been around forever—employee satisfaction."[2] Others believe it's "the willingness to invest discretionary effort on the job."[3] Still others think it's "the employee's connection and commitment to the organization."[4]

Numerous variations increase the confusion about what engagement is and how to get it. Entangling the topic are people targeting engagement outcomes, focusing on employer practices or predictors, or evaluating gaps such as employee commitment, satisfaction, or well-being. As researchers study and measure engagement differently, and organizations evolve definitions to manage and quantify ingredients that matter to their success, it's no wonder differences abound.

It's not this chapter's purpose to debate the approaches or expound on the wealth of research and information on the topic. The goal instead is to make it practical in the real world for you. As such, engagement as a tangible and applicable concept for Trust, Inc. leaders is best captured, I believe, by Professor Thomas Britt of Clemson University and his research colleagues. They define job engagement as *"feeling responsible for and committed to superior job performance, so that job performance 'matters' to the individual."*[5] Bottom line? Engaged people do great work. They're invested in their performance.

Who wouldn't want to lead people who are "committed to superior job performance?" Isn't that a dream for anyone who manages? The question then is this: How do you enable "superior job performance?"

ENGAGING SELF

I was reading in the airport while waiting for a flight to Houston, when a housekeeping employee tidying around me was approached by her supervisor. "You know," he said, "I'd like you to pace yourself." Intrigued by his words, I stopped reading to eavesdrop. "You're doing too good a job. You don't need to work so hard," he told her.

"I like my area clean and looking good for everyone," she said, confused by his direction. "Anyway, I get all my work done." When they parted, her body language was not of relief, but despair. Her disengaged boss's message wasn't about a staff member who needed to work harder to finish her work, but someone setting standards others might not meet.

I hope, despite her boss's attitude, that the engaged housekeeper kept her passion, standards, and vision of an inviting, clean respite for weary travelers. But research hints it's unlikely. According to Dr. Britt, "The more employees care about performance the less they tolerate work conditions that do not allow them to perform at an optimal level."[6] Frustration, stress, dissatisfaction, and even turnover can result.

As a Trust, Inc. leader, it's impossible to engage the unengaged, or keep the engaged engaging, without being engaged yourself. It's unrealistic to think you can create a trust-pocket where others show up and do great work unless you're showing up and doing great work too. And it's unlikely you'll bring a 21st-century work culture of "sustainable engagement," the drivers of which "focus almost entirely on the culture and the relational aspects of the work experience,"[7] to your work group unless you're aware of how your behavior impacts them. Are you enabling or hindering superior performance in those you lead? How engaged are you?

REFLECTIVE EXERCISE
What About Me?

Consider your self-engagement level at work. On a scale of 1 to 5, rate yourself:

         1 = Never

         2 = Rarely

         3 = Sometimes

         4 = Usually

         5 = Almost Always

1. I enjoy what I do.
2. I feel I make a contribution.
3. I like to learn and tackle new challenges.
4. When I commit to a project or deadline, I'm good to my word.
5. I go above and beyond what's expected of me, without prompting.
6. I feel responsible for the work I do.
7. I actively participate in meetings and idea sharing.
8. I take initiative and look for opportunities where I can contribute.
9. I get energized by work-related tasks, projects, or ideas and lose track of time.
10. I like going to work, even on Mondays.
11. I get the information, resources, and support I need to get my job done well.
12. I feel trusted to do my job and, for the most part, am self-governing.

13. I have good working relationships with boss, peers, and staff.
14. Personally, I feel it's fun to do great work.
15. At the end of the day, I feel I've made progress.

Self-scoring: With a score of 60 or above, you can feel confident your self-engaged behaviors provide a positive model to those you lead; with a score of 50 or below, consider that your limited engagement may be negatively impacting staff enthusiasm, discretionary efforts, and results.

Cultivating Self-Engagement

If you're struggling with budget cuts, lack of organizational support, foggy direction, burnout, company politics, immovable roadblocks, or an untrustworthy boss, it's hard to be engaged and "committed to superior performance." Typical responses from highly engaged people to prolonged events such as these, or to unsupportive environments with little hope for short-term improvement, can include: emotional disconnection, reduced loyalty or commitment, withdrawal of discretionary effort, low morale, and increased frustration, stress, and dissatisfaction, often culminating in a decision to find an environment more conducive to self-engagement.[8]

Luckily, most of us don't have all these at once. But we do experience an ebb and flow of engagement levels based on work dynamics and pressures. The challenge remains: If we're to engage the unengaged or positively affect those we lead we must learn how to manage our own engagement. We must do this throughout and despite organizational change, career setbacks, fluctuating workloads, challenging bosses, and difficult peers. Doing that requires approaches for personal growth and well-being that foster self-engagement. Following are a few of those approaches.

❖ **Leverage competence.** Operating with energy and enthusiasm can become a distant memory when a favorite project is eliminated, responsibilities are piled on, or a shift in direction or leadership occurs. Recommitting to a strengths strategy offers insight on how to heighten your engagement. What do you and your team do exceptionally well? What are the strengths you have as individuals, and as a group? How can you leverage these talents to meet the challenge? Research confirms that employees experience higher engagement and performance when strengths are emphasized.[9] Tapping collective competence can make this a time of exceptional growth and opportunity for both you and the team.

❖ **Remain other-focused.** Most of us don't have the power to stop muddy, messy, confusing times at work pushing us toward disengagement. But we do have power to create clarity for staff. Part of a leader's role is managing through the work stuff, good and not so good. My 20 years in management taught me this: acknowledge it, then assist others in finding their way through it. When you help others, you help yourself. By focusing on how you can make it easier, better, or clearer for people you lead to do their work, you stay engaged. In the words of Daniel Goleman, author of *Emotional Intelligence*, "When we focus on others, our world expands. Our own problems drift to the periphery of the mind and so seem smaller, and we increase our capacity for connection—or compassionate action."

❖ **Link to purpose.** I've used this to reboot my self-engagement hundreds of times, but it requires having a purpose, or dream. When our little-self gets stuck, defeated, or emotionally bruised, and we disconnect effort or commitment, tap a bigger-self—the one who passionately wants to makes a difference, contribute to a larger world, or achieve a lifelong dream. You may be inspired by your organization's mission, your vision for your life's work, your role as a parent or community fundraiser, or that product idea or novel you work on on weekends. It doesn't matter what it is, only that it is. Working toward a heart-connected purpose or an aspirational dream can restore your well-being and re-engage the best of who you are.

Gallup research found that "Direct reports of supervisors with thriving wellbeing were 15% more likely to be thriving six months later." According to that same research, "a certain level of trust needs to be built before the wellbeing of supervisors can rub off on their team, whereas peers can have an immediate influence."[10]

Do you love coming to work? Enjoy being a boss? Like the challenge of your workday? Are you committed to your superior performance? Guess what—your staff knows those answers and it rubs off on them. In the words of management expert Ken Blanchard, "If you want to know why your people are not performing well, step up to the mirror and take a peek."

ENGAGING OTHERS

If engagement were as simple as motivational folklore expounds, then pithy sayings, ping-pong tables, tangible rewards, and constant recognition would not just prevail, but work. However, engagement can't be bought.

The message is two-fold. First, the way to engage others is by creating a trusting environment where people can be self-engaged. Second, *lack of engagement is the symptom, not the problem*. Although talent management and organizational development goals seek engagement as the solution to diminished employee commitment, reduced discretionary efforts, and flat-lined creativity, *the problem is distrust*, not engagement. If you want engagement, you need trust. I want to be clear: Trust doesn't cause engagement, but is a requirement for it. When trust is lacking, disengagement results.[11] It works this way: "Leaders create trust in followers, and it is the trust followers experience that enables behavioral engagement."[12]

Leaders who get the best results aren't focused on engagement; they're focused on trust. They build winning trust-cultures where people are self-engaged; where people contribute, innovate, and passionately bring their best to their work. This doesn't mean there aren't additional contributors to, or conditions for, engagement—there are. But, trust is essential.

In a TED Talk, author Daniel Pink highlighted the "mismatch between what science knows and what business does."[13] Unfortunately, most leaders still operate with last century's knowledge of motivation and engagement. But those who build trust currency and foster engagement understand what works in today's workplace.

Motivation and Other Workplace Myths

In many of my workshops where workplace myths and truths are discussed, it's interesting to listen to human resource professionals and seasoned leaders debate what they "know" as the biggest motivators at work. Money. Recognition. Flexibility. Interesting work. Feedback. Goals. Incentives. Autonomy. These answers are typical. But the truth is none is the top motivator.

Research led by Harvard Professor Teresa Amabile unearthed today's top motivator of performance: "making progress on meaningful work."[14] When hurdles, bureaucracy, and wheel-spinning block meaningful accomplishment, motivation is blocked too. But motivation soars when people sail through obstacles and make progress on work that matters.

Just knowing that simple truth opens doors to how you can enable engagement and self-motivation in your work group—you can facilitate their progress. Making a decision, cutting through red tape, clarifying conflicting priorities, or providing needed input can spur motivation and progress. Plus, you'll build trust. When your behavior demonstrates a positive intention of helpfulness, that is trust-building.

The way we get information, do work, and collaborate is vastly different from the way it was even a decade ago. So are expectations about work, work approaches, and workplaces. Following is a sampling of what's changed and changing in the new workplace. Like technology, there will always be something new—some new research, process improvement, or thinking that swirls headlines and ignites consultants. But not everything new is better, nor everything old outdated. The key for Trust, Inc. leaders is leading from a personal state of curiosity, interest, and passion. That requires staying open, interested, and relevant.

The Way It Was	The Way It's Moving
Influence came with a title	Not about title, but behavior
One size fits most; minimize differences; "fair" means equal	Make it personalized; customize; differences okay
Top-down; command and control; management knows best	Local culture–focused; foster engagement and self-motivation; self-governing
Employees as "assets"; human resources; human capital	People as partners, colleagues, collaborators, innovators, problem-solvers
Need-to-know; prepackaged and approved communications	Thoughtful transparency; shared information; voices rising

Change starts from the top	Change starts from anywhere
Lead and manage by short-term goals, longer-term objectives, or vision	Inspire with purpose; endurance of something significant; legacy; making a difference in the world

The interaction between people and their environment creates the psychological process called "motivation." Author Daniel Pink sums it up in his book *Drive*: "The science shows that the secret to high performance isn't our biological drive or our reward-and-punishment drive, but our third drive—our deep-seated desire to direct our own lives, to extend and expand our abilities, and to live a life of purpose."[15]

One Culture Does Not Engage All

Some people like command-and-control environments; others prefer results-only work or high autonomy. Some thrive in highly competitive, silo-filled, win cultures; others excel in collaborative winning cultures sharing ideas and information. Some find structure stifling; others feel it's essential. Our differences drive our likes and dislikes. Traits, personalities, strengths, aspirations, and backgrounds influence what we find best suited for us. There's no one culture or management style that's engaging to everyone.

What's a boss to do? Increase your odds by developing a culture conducive to self-motivation and engagement with these tips:

❖ **Accept your role.** You're not responsible for motivating others. You are, however, responsible for creating a work culture in which people can be self-motivated. Engagement evolves from an inner process. Your role is to *enable* it. That means seeing and treating people as unique, recognizing and using their strengths, and supporting and encouraging individual-ized development. View yourself not as a manager of people or processes but as an enabler of talents; a catalyst for great work.

❖ **Find your grounding.** It's common in sessions with young leaders to field questions about how to gain respect, or how to lead experienced people. It's common with seasoned lead-ers to hear questions about the next generation—How do I connect with the X-ers, Y-ers, or Z-ers? The answer is the same: Find your grounding. When people know who you are, not who they want you to be, or who you want them to think you are, the dynamic shifts to authenticity. Know your values, strengths, hot buttons, aspirations, needs, wants, limitations, and passions. Know what matters to you, in the big scheme of things. Lead from there.

❖ **Start with trust.** Unlocking engagement starts with trust. It's the chicken and the egg: Trusted relationships fuel en-gagement; engagement fuels trust. These words from Chris Hitch, program director at the University of North Carolina's Kenan-Flagler Business School, captures this essential for bosses (the italics are mine): "Unfortunately, many senior leaders cannot seem to shake the top-down model of man-agement that adheres to the notion that authority creates trust. *In reality, trust creates authority.*"[16] Trust also creates work groups with creative innovation, high productivity, superior performance, and exceptional results.

Aspirational Jolts

It doesn't have to be a horizons-expanding declaration—"landing a man on the moon and returning him safely to the earth by the end of the decade," as President John F. Kennedy challenged in 1961. It doesn't have to be an industry-changing product—as Steve Jobs and Apple achieved with the iPod. And it doesn't even have to be a visionary, organization-wide initiative—to which author Jim Collins refers in *Built to Last* as "Big Hairy Audacious Goals (BHAG)."

Any of these works as an aspirational jolt, but in Trust, Inc., think smaller. Putting on a conference, handling an important project, opening a new office, or creating a prototype might all be aspirational jolts. In one of my corporate roles, starting a new subsidiary was one for my team. So were smaller jolts such as designing an awards program, starting a new department, piloting a marketing idea, or hiring hundreds in a few weeks.

Sometime jolts come as delegated tasks, which may or may not generate engagement. But aspirational jolts are often team-initiated or team-evolved ideas that gain momentum, and are tied to a broader purpose. In this context, aspirational jolts are things you and/or your team can control, manage, and finish.

The reason they're aspirational is that they challenge you and your staff. They push time frames, resources, creativity, or relationships. They also develop know-how, confidence, accountability, and trust. I've learned a few things about aspirational jolts from a management perspective:

1. Engagement flourishes when the desired outcome is doable, but not easy.

2. Encourage jolts by saying yes whenever possible to others' ideas, assuming they have performance trust—i.e., they can do what they say they can do.

3. Celebrate achievement and risk taking; help people see what it looks like to be successful on your team.

4. Bigger doesn't mean better. Some jolts might be completed in a few days. It's the doing that engages and inspires superior performance.

5. Bet on passion. People who are passionate about an idea, a problem, or a solution thrive with aspirational jolts. Let them.

This powerful and simple approach requires no budget approval or permission. In fact, self-engaged people regularly set aspirational jolts for themselves.

WATCH OUT FOR THOSE PLAQUES!

"Employees are our most important asset."

"The best employees work here."

"Our values are at the heart of everything we do."

At first glance, these words seem innocuous. For many of us, they represent an ideal version of who we'd like to be at our best, or our hope of how we'd really like it to be. But plaques touting people as the most important asset are trust-killers—unless you work in the small percentage of companies where that's actually true. Messages on department walls touting wishful thinking versus real actions diminish credibility and trust. Take them down.

When our "most important assets" are disposable in a challenged economy, are required to do more with less year after year, or go without increases against the backdrop of executive bonuses, the words are a reminder of failed promises.

When poor performers continue collecting paychecks despite poor performance, making it harder for those who work with them to get their work done, the cynic in all of us asks, "Really? The best employees work here?"

When the latest management promotion is known for dark-side company politics and silo mentality, it's hard to believe an engraved plaque professing the values of teamwork and communication is "at the heart of everything we do."

And when a store owner lectures on the importance of excellent customer service, but consistently under-staffs peak hours, she reduces staff engagement. That disconnect between what is said and done diminishes trust.

Behavioral integrity is the alignment between words and actions, and is one of five trust essentials we'll explore in Part II. In the words of Tony Simons, Cornell associate professor, "Behavioral integrity is not about some higher moral code. It is simply about having words and actions reflect each other. The more employees see their managers as having that kind of integrity, the more committed they become to the company."[17]

Whereas the word–action disconnect is a trust-buster, their connection is a trust-builder. If, instead of taking those plaques down, you want to make their promises a reality for your Trust, Inc., start here:

❖ **Decide what those words "look like" for your group.** What does it mean to be treated as "the most important asset," or operate with values as the "heart of everything we do" around here? What does it look like to demonstrate a particular organizational philosophy, value, or goal in your department? By making the words seeable with specific behaviors, the word–action alignment becomes more doable. This allows staff to gain an understanding of how their boss (you) should be expected to operate toward them, and how they should operate with each other.

❖ **Reward behaviors that demonstrate a word–action connection.** What are you rewarding in your staff? How are their results aligned with those messages on the wall? If you want integrity in your work group, don't promote people who don't have it. If information-sharing and collaboration is an organizational value, incorporate regular feedback about these practices into discussions.

❖ **Integrate the what and the how.** What you do is different from how you do it. You can deliver great results, but your approach may diminish morale or another's trust in the process. Who enables your superior performance—someone using bullying techniques, intimidating approaches, lying, and manipulation, or someone offering the best of who they are to their work? Those who build trust know that *how* they do *what* they do matters. To them, it's not a sometimes approach; it's their all-the-time style.

❖   **Acknowledge discrepancies.** You may not be able to re-
    move that plaque, or change the performance/reward system
    where you work to shape and nudge trust-building behav-
    iors, but you can create your trust-pocket where those mes-
    sages are true. Start fresh by acknowledging where things are
    now and your desire to move toward these concepts. Use
    the discrepancies between what is and what could be as an
    honest and transparent discussion. Begin the dialogue with
    what matters around here.

Plaques of unfulfilled promises aren't the cause of workplace
disengagement or distrust; they're a reminder of yesterday's missed
alignment and failed ideas. But as a Trust, Inc. leader, you know it
doesn't have to be that way. Engagement, as is trust, is a local issue.
In the words of South African social rights activist Desmond Tutu,
"You make a difference where you are."

CHAPTER 3

Be a Trusted Boss

The only person you are destined to become is the person you decide to be.

~ Ralph Waldo Emerson

Seated in the courtyard of a sports bar during a playoff game in the home city of one of the teams, I was part of an energetic crowd that Sunday. Although we'd come for something quick to eat, we caught glimpses of a play now and then as home-team enthusiasts roared approval during the first half.

When a man sat next to us with two friends, ordered a pitcher of beer, and maneuvered around to glimpse the game, we barely noticed. But when he hassled the waitress every few minutes trying to intimidate her into getting him a table closer to the TV when none existed, his rudeness and her discomfort drew our attention.

Growing increasingly agitated at not being able to watch the football game from inside the bar, the man stood up after 20 minutes, ordered his colleagues up, and walked away without paying. It wasn't just the beer he stole. That thief stole the waitress's well-being. Fighting back tears as she explained what happened to her manager, the customer's action left a big impact.

Across the country there are similar workplace heists. Yes, there's the shoplifting variety, but those causing lasting damage are not as blatant. These involve emotional thievery, diminished trust, reduced happiness, and decreased self-esteem.

When a boss steals an idea from a staff member without acknowledging his contribution, she diminishes his trust. When a manager continually sets unrealistic deadlines without concern for a workload that robs his nights and weekends, she reduces his commitment. And when a leader sends reactive e-mails or texts harsh critiques without reflective pause, she ravages self-esteem.

We remember bosses who cause emotional heists and diminish trust. But when we're in charge, it can be difficult to see how our actions impact others. Hence this chapter. Consider it a two-sided mirror—one side offering a glimpse of behaviors that enhance trust, the other showing those that diminish it.

As we know from Towers Watson's research, the number-one quality people want in workplace leaders is trustworthiness.[1] But what does it mean to be a boss worthy of someone's trust? What do people need from you in order to trust you? Although your staff might like to tell you, they probably won't. Studies confirm more than 50 percent of employees are afraid to speak up at work.[2] This chapter is their proxy. It's a composite of what any staff would like for *any* boss to know about being trusted.

The first thing a staff wants you to know about how they perceive your trustworthiness is this: Do you have their interests in mind? Are you looking out for them? Their interpretation of your actions drives this perception of your trustworthiness.

According to University of Minnesota researchers, "'Trustworthy' means one is *able and willing* to act in the other person's best interests."[3] A sense of "trustworthy" is derived from perceptions or beliefs about five categories of management behavior: "behavioral consistency, behavioral integrity, sharing and delegation of control, communication, and demonstration of concern."[4] If your staff uses words such as *competent, honest, credible, considerate,* or *fair* to describe you, the answer is clear. Of course, it's clear with these words too: *clueless, disrespectful, self-absorbed, out of touch,* or *manipulative.* What do people say about you? True or not true, their perception of you is *their* reality.

THE HARD FACTS

Research confirms self-blindness. First, we judge ourselves better than others. This "better-than-average effect" blocks self-awareness. We think we're unique or exceptional. Washington University Professor Jonathan D. Brown put it this way: "Among other things, most people believe they are more (a) virtuous, honorable, and moral than others; (b) capable, competent, and talented than others; and (c) compassionate, understanding, and sympathetic than others. People even believe they are more human than others, though less biased and prone to error."[5] And, of course, we drive better!

Second, we exclude ourselves from thinking we're "part of the problem," believing it's others who need to change. Third, we operate with self-serving bias, meaning we're likely to attribute our successes to "internal or personal factors" and our failures to "external or situational factors."[6]

Take the external factor of the Great Recession. Some consider it as *the* reason trust is at an all-time low between leaders and followers, stopping short of any self-reflection. When the economy improves, so will trust, right? Don't count on it. In the majority of workplaces, the trust deficiency has been decades in the making. Factors involved in building or diminishing trust are multidimensional and complex. Although the Great Recession did significantly impact trust, it's not the reason someone wouldn't be perceived as a trusted boss by his or her team. Remember, trust is a local issue (see the Intro for more on why). According to Andy Atkins, Director of Research and Development for the *Leadership, Collaboration, and Trust Research Report*, "Even as employees express trust in peers by saying they share and collaborate more easily with colleagues, employees remain wary and distrustful of their leaders."[7]

You may think you're different from those "other leaders," and perhaps you are, but the reality is we perceive ourselves as trusting and trustworthy, whereas others don't necessarily perceive us that way. Self-blindness should give any boss wanting to be a trusted leader pause, especially against these findings:

- Only 18 percent of people believe a "business or governmental leader will actually tell the truth when confronted with a difficult issue."[8]

- "Only 14 percent believe their company leaders are ethical and honest."[9]

- Just 11 percent of organizations "foster high-trust environments where employees are encouraged to take risks, make decisions, and innovate around products, services, and processes."[10]

Hard facts, changing times, and self-blindness make self-reflection and self-challenging a good habit. As Arthur H. Sulzberger, mid-20th-century publisher of *The New York Times* wrote, "For 11 months and maybe about 20 days each year we concentrate upon the shortcomings of others, but for a few days, at the turn of New Year we look at our own. It is a good habit." It's an essential one for trusted bosses.

WHAT YOUR STAFF WANTS YOU TO KNOW

In an era of distrust and growing cynicism about those who lead, today is a good day to begin that habit by taking a look through others' eyes. If you're serious about creating your Trust, Inc., reflect on these composite messages from staff:

1. **Don't blame human resources.** Distrust can't be fixed with programs. You don't need a better recognition program—you need to say thank you, send a personalized e-mail, or stop in or call to say you noticed we did exceptional work. You don't need a communication program—you need frequent dialogue that keeps us part of what's happening, not the last to know. And you don't need trust-building training or an employee survey to improve morale or engagement—you need to treat us like we matter, not in a "corporate assets" way, but as talented, creative, and innovative individuals.

2. **We need each other.** We're not naïve about business or its challenges. We know there are problems with *some* bosses and *some* staff. But finger-pointing, blaming, and perpetuating an "us vs. them" mentality exacerbates it. Bottom line? We need each other. Distrusting us impacts engagement. Disengagement reduces productivity, results, profits, and jobs. What's needed is a balanced understanding of our mutual worth, and a new start to work relationships founded on mutual benefit.

3. **Reverse your mindset.** When you orient to what's wrong rather than what's right, you communicate distrust to us. It's backward to write rules, limit sound practices, and make short-term decisions with long-term impact around a delinquent few. That communicates distrust to the 90-plus percent who are committed, trustworthy, and hard working. Shift your mindset. Design processes and policies for trustworthy people who are as committed to their jobs as you are to yours. If you can't trust the people who work for you, why are they working for you?

4. **Own your part.** We understand you're under pressure to meet goals and quarterly objectives, but you're killing our initiative with terse e-mails and escalated demands. Refrains such as "just make it happen" or "I don't care what it takes," or a command-and-control style won't yield the results you seek. Neither will shallow, generic praise about us being

"key players" or "important to the overall results." Your actions communicate what you think. Each day, you make a choice to trust or not trust; engage or not engage; respect or not respect.

5. **Model your messages.** Remember eliminating Business Class for international travel from the department's budget, but exempting yourself and select others from it? Or those "all hands on deck" Saturdays you mandated to meet a deadline, but you disappeared after a few hours? Well, we noticed. When what you say and do aren't in alignment, you lose credibility. No credibility = no trust. Start there.

But wait! There's good news about the impact you can have when you're a trusted boss. British Columbia University economists found that moving up just one point on a 10-point scale of trust in management boosts "overall satisfaction in life by about the same amount as a 36-percent raise would."[11] Want to boost your staff's overall satisfaction and well-being without spending a cent? You can. Part II explores the needed essentials to boost your management-trust scale with your staff.

EVERYDAY BEHAVIORS

Most of us want to be perceived as trustworthy. We want to work in winning cultures and operate with trust. But could common behaviors be reducing trust without you knowing it? Or are you helping it flourish with trusted-boss actions? Consider the following trust-diminishing and -enhancing behaviors. Which are more reflective of how you operate?

Behaviors That Diminish Trust

Lying is the number-one behavior that diminishes trust. It also tops the list of what people say when they think of trust betrayed. No surprise. But you don't need to lie, deceive, or manipulate to diminish trust. Operating in rote mode or with impaired self-aware-ness, you can diminish trust with ordinary, everyday behaviors:

- **You over-promise and under-deliver.** Some call it hype, others reference the saying "all hat, no cattle," but the yield is the same. If you don't take your words seriously, why would someone trust them?

- **You operate as if others can't be trusted.** Your communication approach, delegation style, and procedural mandates broadcast your view of others. Distrust is not the opposite of trust, control is.

- **You relinquish personal accountability.** Blaming others. Not apologizing. Being a victim. Offering excuses. These aren't trust-enhancing behaviors. People who own their actions build trust; people who don't, diminish it.

- **You escalate the e-mail chain, hitting Reply All and CC-ing your boss and his boss.** Adding the boss and the boss's boss and everyone in between screams distrust. A cover-your-you-know-what style ignites contagious distrust.

- **You take credit without acknowledging others' contributions.** You may think you did it alone, worked the hardest, or came up with the idea. But others influenced, helped, and supported you. Not recognizing that reduces trust; knowing and not acknowledging it batters it.

- **You tell half-truths, and use spin, avoidance, and weasel words.** Deliberately opaque, misleading, or evasive communication offers a kind of transparency—one spotlighting character. Communications not grounded in integrity, forthrightness, and honesty impact trust.

- **You visit the dark side of company politics.** Whether it's telling "gotcha" stories, escalating unhealthy conflict, or operating with a "win" versus "winning" philosophy, those who serve politics at work with other-than-honorable intentions reduce trust.

- **You choose e-mail or text message, or delegate the delivery of difficult messages.** How you handle the difficult communication is, itself, a message. Hiding behind one-way communication, or relinquishing involvement, is a trust-buster.

- **You bypass the person involved.** Not happy with something someone did or didn't do, so you told everyone but him? Jumped over the person heading the project in order to get something changed, and didn't include her in the process? It's trust-destroying.

- **You lack self-awareness.** When words are biting, e-mails and texts are written as personal attacks, or work relationships are viewed as easily changeable, trust diminishes. Those who lack self-awareness about how their actions are perceived by others risk operating without trust currency.

These are just a few trust-diminishing behaviors; I'm sure you can name dozens more. If you want to operate with trust and build a trust-pocket, pay attention to yourself. Start with your intentions, actions, commitments, and behaviors. We want *others* to be truthful, operate in trustworthy ways, and demonstrate alignment between words and actions. Here's the twist: We're more likely to get what we want from others if we operate that way ourselves and eliminate our own trust-busting behaviors.

Behaviors That Enhance Trust

Look around any organization and you'll see trust. There's some division, department, work unit, or team where people shine, ideas flourish, and exceptional work is achieved. We can all learn from these trust-pockets and the formal and informal leaders who ignite that trust. So, what does a trusted boss look like? Their trust-enhancing behaviors go beyond the basics. Here's a sampling:

- **They're good at what they do.** The competent performance of your job is a litmus test for believability. Competence builds performance trust. Content may be king on the Internet, but competence is king at work.

- **They're passionate about their work.** Passion isn't cheerleading, platitudes, or crank-it-up faux enthusiasm. It comes from an inner desire, determination, and drive. For many, it's making a difference or contributing to the whole. It shows up softly in some leaders, loudly in others, but it's easily discernible by anyone around them.

- **They care about people.** They're kind and considerate, operating with a compassionate and benevolent heart. They see people as individuals, without gender, generational, or stereotypical biases.

- **They want the best for you.** They bring out the best in others, and help them apply and develop their strengths and reach their goals. They provide challenges and opportunities to help you go where *you* want to go. They want to make the pie bigger so everyone can be successful.

- **They listen.** They don't listen so they can talk; they listen so they can learn. By withholding judgment, being present, and engaging real dialogue, they embrace differences, create openness, and facilitate connection.

- **They operate with self-awareness.** They pay attention to their words and actions. They don't commit what they can't control, make promises they can't keep, or fail to own mistakes or shortcomings.

- **They have perspective.** Certainly there are crises at work, but these leaders don't yell *Fire!* at every hiccup or problem. They step back before sounding the alarm, put setbacks in context, and understand that despite big efforts, things don't always turn out as planned. In the real world of what matters in life, trusted leaders keep perspective.

- **They manage direction and work, not people.** They paint word-pictures to help people see the end vision, or "what it looks like" to hit the target. They leave the fun in work by setting direction, not dictating details. They clear hurdles, reduce bureaucracy, and make it easier, not harder, for people to get their work done.

- **They say thank you.** They appreciate, value, and acknowledge the efforts and contributions of those they work with. In the words of Arnold H. Glasgow, "A good leader takes a little more than his share of the blame; a little less than his share of the credit."

- **They see beyond self.** It's not about *their* promotion, bonus, or achievement; it's about something bigger. They link the why behind the what, and help others view the landscape with purpose. We all need a reason to get up in the morning. These people enable us to see why and how our work does indeed matter.

Trusted bosses nurture and grow trust in a variety of ways, but one thing is certain: They're magnets for the best talent, ideas, and contributions. They understand that the way to help people bring their talents to work is to create an emotionally safe, consistently caring, and dependably open trust-pocket, or winning culture, founded on authentic trust. Authentic trust comes from authentic people (see Chapter 9).

Trusted bosses look in the mirror. One way to start looking in the mirror is to see what's reflected by others. When you can identify what you need from your boss, you're likely to glimpse what others need from you. Take a look.

REFLECTIVE THINKING
What Do You Want From Your Boss?

Writing responses can enhance self-awareness. Only consider answers related to your intangible needs (for example, transparent communication is intangible; a bigger budget is tangible).

What do I need from my boss that I'm not getting that...

1. would enable me to feel trusted, or more trusted?

2. would enhance the quality of my work or increase my results?

3. would make it easier for me to create a trust-pocket?

Furthermore...

1. Is my boss *able* to provide me the elements I said were missing in 1, 2, and 3? If so, which? Is he *willing*? Have I ever told him?

2. Am I giving these same elements, the ones I'm missing from my boss, to my staff? If not, why not? Am I willing? Am I able?

Similar to myself, you've probably worked for bosses you trusted and bosses you didn't. But here's what Trust, Inc. leaders know: Being a trusted boss has nothing to do with whether or not *you* work for one. Trust currency is not a generic currency that passes freely from one person to any other. It's creator-specific. You create your own currency by giving authentic trust. You can't borrow or invest someone else's trust. If your boss is not investing trust currency in you, don't let that impact how you create and invest trust in your staff.

RESPECTED OR LIKED?

We like to be liked. Just look at the ubiquitous "like" symbol from Facebook. However, trusted bosses know that being liked isn't what builds trust; being respected is. The type of respect that builds work trust goes beyond "categorical respect," as postulated by the philosopher Immanuel Kant, which finds that "all people are due respect by virtue of being moral agents and reasoning beings."[12] To be a trusted leader, you need an additional kind of respect, one called "contingent respect," which affords "status or standing within a group."

According to University of Massachusetts Professor Ronnie Janoff-Bulman, "We are motivated to find the best people within the group to provide guidance, information, and direction. These are the people who are most respected, the individuals granted the strongest voice and most influence over the group."[13] This may or may not be the boss. But, to create and sustain a trust-pocket, you'll need respect.

Although you may have your staff's best interests in mind, *being* trustworthy means you are *willing* and *able* to operate with those interests. How are you viewed by *your* boss and peers? Do they trust you? If not, your organizational clout (the ability to use influence and credibility to get things done on behalf of your staff) will suffer.

I've had bosses I liked, with whom I enjoyed having a drink after work. I've had bosses I respected, with whom I couldn't imagine having a social encounter outside of work. And I've had those I both liked and respected. Although having both is nice, liking doesn't equal trusting. People don't need to like a boss to trust him, but they won't trust him unless they respect him.

Trusted bosses don't make decisions so staff will "like" them; they make decisions because it's the right, fair, and best thing to do. They don't sugarcoat feedback to be "liked"; they provide meaningful critique and input to achieve great results, while encouraging personal and professional growth. They don't hire or promote because they "like" someone; they select the best person who brings the skills needed.

I know how hard it is to be a boss, and how lonely it can feel making hard calls on staff reductions, budget cuts, or the termination of poor performers; how challenging it can be to keep information confidential when you'd like to share it; how gut-wrenching saying no is when you'd like to say yes. However, trusted bosses know that difficult calls enhance respect, credibility, and trust when they're grounded in best-self characteristics such as ethics, integrity, fairness, tolerance, and compassion.

When pressures and people outside your control impact your ability to do what you'd like to do, and you still operate with honesty and integrity, you earn respect. When you're pushed to cross a boundary of what's right and instead push back with courage, you earn respect. When you stand up for what you're *for*, and work passionately to make things better, you earn respect. No one ever said being a trusted boss is easy. But if you're lucky, people may "like" you too.

THE BEST VERSION

I'm not proud to admit I have a temper. People who know me well have seen its head rear if I'm significantly exhausted, extremely stressed, inordinately frustrated with things I can't control, or feeling unheard about something important to me. For those who don't know me well, it's unlikely they'd suspect my capability for volcanic behavior. Either way, my temper has been tempered. It has vastly improved from those 20- and 30-something days of slamming doors or driving away angry. Today, it's a rare occurrence I'm still working to make rarer.

The process of me tracking my temper eruptions and focusing on reduction started from an encounter with a paperweight in a catalog, which read, *Believe in the best version of yourself.* Today that paperweight sits on my desk, because I found the thought provoking. What was my best version? If I could see myself operating *sometimes* under a best-version scenario, couldn't I increase my odds of being *more her*, more often? Maybe it's not all the time I'll have a cool temper, but *more* of the time.

Those paperweight words helped me understand it's the belief in a better way that helps me create that way. I know my best version happens when I'm rested, don't allow little things I can't control to stress me, view events from a what-*really*-matters perspective, and don't take myself too seriously. It also emerges when I'm kinder, more considerate, and inner-connected; when I'm grateful for what I have, not worried about what I don't; when my heart is open, my mind nonjudgmental, and my expectations in check.

Why wouldn't I want to believe in a best version of myself and attempt to actualize her more often? Isn't that what life challenges all of us to do? To live the best of who we are? What can any of us give this world, if not that? What best version of you is waiting in your shadow to be engaged, renewed, and enjoyed by those your life touches?

REFLECTIVE THINKING
The Best You

Consider these questions. Writing your answers can increase insights.

1. What does it "look like" when you're at your best?

2. How would you describe the best version of you?

3. What are you doing when you're at your best?

4. What triggers your best version to be replaced with a worse or lesser version?

5. What can you do to have the best version of you around more often?

If you're not operating as a trusted boss all of the time, then try it some of the time. If you slip into some of those trust-diminishing behaviors under pressure, then pick one at a time to focus on. If you're having challenges making the transition from being liked to being respected, "no worries," as those much younger than me would say. When setbacks happen, and they *always* will, believe in the best version of you.

CHAPTER 4

Trust Others

There is the risk you cannot afford to take and there is the risk you cannot afford not to take.

~ Peter Drucker

Do you trust your staff to work from home, use the Internet professionally, or make good decisions on behalf of customers? Or do you advocate tracking employee Website visits, application usage, or message history? Perhaps you'd like to restrict Web access altogether or at least for certain levels, or have GPS tracking on employee phones to confirm they're where they say they are? What message are your actions sending: I basically trust you, or I don't?

Trust, or the perceived sense of trust, impacts behavior—a fact I once witnessed while on vacation, in line to pay for a gift. I waited while the cashier called the store owner to get permission for a $1.87 refund for the customer in front of me. After receiving an okay the clerk informed us with a rant that if she didn't call for permission she'd be "written up." She demonstrated to a packed store in a popular tourist destination not only how distrusting her boss was, but also her growing contempt for the job.

As an employee, if you believe you're trusted or believe you aren't, it matters. We know there's impact when bosses aren't trusted, but the question we should ask is, What's the impact when bosses don't trust employees? Or when management gives employees that perception? This chapter explores that issue, and highlights elements that get in the way of trusting others.

The reality is you can't create a sustainable trust-pocket without trusting others, nor can you garner enough respect and influence to protect your team without trusting beyond your trust-pocket. Vertical trust. Horizontal trust. You need both. Still, the thought of trusting others should give you pause. Authentic trust is not blind trust. Nor is it absolute or unconditional. Trusting comes with risk.

WHAT RESULTS ARE YOU GETTING?

Amy Lyman, author of *The Trustworthy Leader* and cofounder of the Great Place to Work® Institute, concludes from research on the 100 Best Companies to work for, that "Companies whose employees praise high levels of trust in their workplace are, in fact, among the highest performers, beating average annualized returns of the S&P 500 by a factor of three."[1]

Your local trust-culture has impact. Here are a few ways to quantify the trust currency dividends you make:

- Heightened customer service.
- Decreased turnover of top performers.
- Higher employee engagement.
- Well-being of staff.

- Less interest in unionization.
- More collaboration and teamwork.
- Enhanced creativity and innovation.
- Greater productivity.
- Better relationships.
- Reduced absenteeism and HR-related issues.
- Great work and superior results.

There's a reality in the new workplace: Creating a winning local culture founded on authentic trust is not a "nice to do." It's a strategic imperative for anyone desiring sustainable results and career success.

For Better: Collective Felt Trust

Research from British Columbia professors Sabrina Salamon and Sandra Robinson identified, "When employees in an organization perceive they are trusted by management, increases in the presence of responsibility norms, as well as in the sales performance and customer service performance of the organization, are observed."[2] Their study involving 88 retail stores found, "In stores where employees felt trusted, they were more likely to rise to managers' expectations and perform better in terms of sales and customer service."[3]

When people perceive their manager trusts them, what researchers label "collective felt trust," better behaviors happens. When people feel trusted, they're more likely to accept responsibility, and take actions in support of organizational goals. Nineteenth-century educator Booker T. Washington said, "Few things help an individual more than to place responsibility upon him, and to let him know that you trust him." His words are just as important today.

<u>REFLECTIVE THINKING</u>
What Trust Impressions Are You Giving Your Staff?

Writing your thoughts can enhance self-awareness and insights.

1. How many issues or problems need to be run by you? Why?

2. Do you say "Use your good judgment" to handle a problem? Why or why not?

3. Are your policies and procedures designed to enable work, or to control behavior? What message does this send staff?

4. With whom do you spend the most time: those doing great work, or those who don't? Why? What might you be reinforcing?

5. Think about your total team. On a scale from 1 to 10, with 10 being "without reservation" and 1 being "not at all," how much do you trust your staff to make good decisions in support of your objectives and goals? What happens when you take vacation or aren't reachable?

6. What words describe the work environment you've created? Now step into your staff's shoes. If you worked for you, how would you describe it? Is there felt trust? If not, what can you do to create it?

Self-discovery: Your answers should provide a glimpse of impressions you're leaving. If these aren't the ones you want your team to have, consider how you can adjust your behavior.

Authentic trust that creates trust currency is about relationships. By definition, trust as a relationship builder means there's more than one side. If you're only concerned with whether employees trust you, you're missing the rest of the equation.

For Worse: Collective Felt Fear

I'm not naïve about work, workplaces, or people. I've worked around and with people who created work groups fraught with fear, layered with intense control, reeking of dark-side politics, and dense with adult bullying styles. Some entire organizations have a palpable negative culture. Author Liz Ryan notes, "The principal signs of a fear-soaked senior leadership are a preoccupation with looking out for No.1, a clampdown on consensus-building conversations, and the shunning or ousting of anyone so bold or naïve as to tell the truth about what he or she believes."[4]

Fear, according to Webster, is an emotion caused by "an anticipation or awareness of danger." Working in cultures fueled by intimidation, secrecy, back-stabbing, suspicion, surveillance, and control creates the equivalent of collective felt fear. In these workplaces, danger lurks behind any e-mail, meeting, conversation, or decision.

In his book *Trust: A New View of Personal and Organizational Development*, Jack R. Gibb explains, "Trust and fear are keys to understanding persons and social systems. They are primary and catalytic factors in all human living. When trust is high, relative to fear, people and people systems function well. When fear is high, relative to trust, they break down."[5]

A *Businessweek* story, "The Meanest Company in America," about founder and Chairman of Dish Network, Charlie Ergen, got my attention. Here's one example of that culture: Fingerprint scanners are used for building entry. "If a worker is late, an e-mail is immediately sent to human resources, which then sends another to that person's boss, and sometimes directly to Ergen."[6] Even after working through the night on business problems from home, executives arriving "a few minutes late" were publically berated. Distrust, condescension, and poisonous are words employees used to describe it. The company was ranked the "worst company to work for in America" by the website 24/7 Wall St.

Don't be fooled: Bad cultures don't always mean bad results. The reality about The Dish Network is not that a fear culture destroyed their success, but rather that in five of the last eight Great Recession quarters they beat earnings projections.

If profits for limited shareholders, including oneself, are the goal—for example, taking a startup public just to cash in and move on, or optimizing personal gain without regard to ethical or moral practices—then trust-based cultures fueling sustainable business results for the long term would never be of interest. But companies have different goals and objectives; so do people. Certainly it's easier to build a trust-pocket when your approach and objectives are aligned with those you report to or those who lead your organization. But don't let not having that alignment stop you. In Part III, you'll find tips for trust-pocket building in less than optimal places.

TRUSTING OTHERS BEGINS WITH SELF-TRUST

It's hard to trust at an individual level if you don't trust yourself. Lack of self-trust can be a precursor for distrusting others. Here's why: Researchers found that sharing physical traits with others creates a "perceived attitudinal similarity." In other words, we expect people who appear similar to us (in gender, race, hair color, and so on) to be similar to us.[7] Similarly, if we break our word we think others do too. If you over-promise and under-deliver, you expect the same from others. But if you're trustworthy, you believe those who are "like you" are trustworthy too.

The reality is that although we may perceive others as similar to us, especially in certain industries or professions, and expect them to "act like us," we're quite different. Coworkers arrive in male and female versions, with different ages, races, ethnicities, nationalities, and characteristics, as well as backgrounds, values, interests, and experiences.

Twentieth-century journalist Sydney J. Harris wrote, "It's surprising how many persons go through life without ever recognizing that their feelings toward other people are largely determined by their feelings toward themselves, and if you're not comfortable within yourself, you can't be comfortable with others."[8]

In this increasingly complex world, our ability to judge real or not real, scam or opportunity, credible or not credible, trust or no trust, is a 21st-century necessity. That skill begins with self-trust. Can you trust your motives, impulses, and intentions? Do you lie to yourself? Do you break self-promises? Do you trust your judgment when giving trust to others? If you want to trust others, start by building trust with yourself.

Practical Truths About Self-Trust

- **Self-trust involves trusting your intentions, motives, and integrity.** It includes reliance on self and confidence in self-actions. But it goes deeper. Self-trust is "the ability to trust one's self to trust wisely and authentically," according to authors Robert Solomon and Fernando Flores.[9] Self-trust is grounded in self-awareness, well-intentioned and consistent behavior, and commitments honored and fulfilled. You're unlikely to be viewed by others as trustworthy if you don't view yourself that way. And you're unlikely to view yourself that way if you're not that way.

- **Self-trust is a skill that fuels accountability.** Self-trust is a tenet of accountability. When we hold ourselves accountable for our actions, decisions, choices, words, and behaviors we build self-trust. Building self-trust requires self-awareness. That means there's a self-initiated, account-giving relationship between who you say you are and who you are. You grow self-trust when you have alignment among what you value, say, and do. That demonstrates trustworthiness to yourself.

- **Self-trust involves being in your own corner.** Self-care and self-support enable self-trust. When you limit critical and demeaning mind-talk, accept an imperfect you, treat yourself as a dear friend, and don't betray who you are for others, self-trust grows. Self-trust is not an age-of-me narcissistic self-absorption, but acts in the spirit of putting your oxygen mask on first before helping others. Confidence, self-esteem, and resilience grow when you trust yourself. Until you deeply trust yourself, profoundly trusting others will escape your grasp.

- **Self-trust is essential to the most important relationship—the one with self.** A practice of self-trust offers a way to explore your possibilities, gifts, and passions. Self-trust grows the inner path. It aids the discovery of your life's potential. Jack R. Gibb writes, "Trust creates the flow and gentles the mind-body-spirit. When I trust myself I am able to enter fully into the process of discovering and creating who I am. When I trust my own inner process I am able to become what I am meant to become."[10]

Often when I mentor individuals or help managers develop trust-pockets, we start with self-trust. You can't create a thriving work group fueled by authentic trust without including yourself in that trust-building endeavor.

REFLECTIVE EXERCISE
Do You Trust You?

Circle the statements that are true for you at least 85 percent of the time at work.

1. I don't make promises I can't keep.

2. "I don't care what you have to do or how you have to do it" isn't something I'd say. Integrity matters to me.

3. My word is as strong as any contract.

4. I sleep well, knowing I did my best and operated with good intentions.

5. When I make a mistake, even an important one, I own it, learn from it, and move on.

6. I'm honest with myself and others.

7. I speak up when decisions or issues are going down a negative-values path.

8. I reach goals I set for myself.

9. I make well-informed decisions about people and issues.

10. I find time to renew, revitalize, and refresh myself.

Self-discovery: Review any statements not circled and ask, What is going on here for me? How might this affect the trust I'm building with myself? What can I do to better achieve this?

We can betray our own trust, just as others can betray the trust we give them. We can disappoint ourselves by how we show up, compromise integrity, float or be pulled to grey areas. We can let ourselves down by failing to keep a promise or delivering less than best-of-self behaviors. We can be silent when we wish we'd spoken, or ill-intentioned instead of more benevolent. Good people can do stupid things—at least I know I have.

Trusting self means risking the betrayal of that trust on occasion, just as trusting others risks betrayal. We're imperfectly us. Forgiving ourselves and learning from our missteps enhances personal growth. Author Julia Cameron adds perspective on its benefits: "When we trust ourselves, we become more humble and more daring. When we trust ourselves, we move surely."[11] Self-trust enables trusting others.

YOUR BELIEFS ABOUT TRUSTING OTHERS

What are your beliefs about others? Do you think most people are trustworthy or most people aren't? If you believe people can't be trusted, that belief dictates your actions, approaches, and behaviors. If you believe everyone is worthy of your trust and naively give trust according to that belief, without consideration or judgment, you'll find disappointment. Both viewpoints are problematic for those who lead.

Our beliefs affect our decisions—from the halo effect, in which one great trait causes us to generalize an overall positive impression, to the Pygmalion effect, in which we act in accordance with our own expectations, enabling those expectations to come true—the connection between what we expect and what we get is well documented. When it comes to trusting others, we're wise to remember not to believe everything we think, good or not good.

Tips for Harnessing Your Beliefs

❖ **Relinquish assumptions.** Whom do you believe is more engaged and committed to their work—the people you see at work or those who are working remotely? Research nods to remote workers.[12] But our assumptions affect our actions: Despite research findings to the contrary, plenty of bosses don't trust a work-anywhere approach for those whose responsibilities permit. An employer survey found just 20 percent make it possible for employees "to access work material no matter where they are, which includes e-mail, applications and front- and back-office cloud services."[13] Check your assumptions. Are any blocking you from trusting staff or peers?

❖ **Eliminate role bias.** Behaviors, not roles, should be the standard for who receives trust. I once worked for a client who believed salaried employees were trustworthy to receive Internet access, but hourly or non-exempt employees couldn't be trusted. Trusting behaviors are grounded in integrity and positive intention, not assigned by title or role. A doctor or priest may "seem" more trustworthy based on role, but recent history reminds us otherwise.

❖ **Ask.** When we believe we know what others want, attach stereotypic generalizations to ages or genders, or postulate another's desires without inquiring, and then act on what we think we "know," our misperceptions limit trust building. For example, if I decide not to promote you to project lead, believing your family commitments preclude you from being interested in growth opportunities, I'm doing the workplace equivalent of fortune-telling. Why not ask? Research confirms common sense: "The extent to which managers involve employees influence[s] the development of trust."[14] The more staff is involved in decisions that affect them, the higher the trust.

❖ **Be warned!** In *Thinking Fast and Slow*, Nobel Prize winner Daniel Kahneman illuminates decision making this way: "The normal state of your mind is that you have intuitive feelings and opinions about almost everything that comes your way. You like or dislike people long before you know much about them; you trust or distrust strangers without knowing why; you feel that an enterprise is bound to succeed without analyzing it."[15] The problem is what he calls "what you see is all there is." We make decisions on what's in front of us, without expanding our frame of reference. Couple that with "confirmation biases," or the tendency to seek information that agrees with or supports our beliefs. When you're "certain you're right," it's a good time to seek input countering your beliefs. Go beyond what's in front of you.

❖ **Keep perspective.** You can find examples of untrustworthy people, broken promises, and trust-busting actions, but keep perspective. When headlines scream "STEROID-TAKING ATHLETES," "TEACHERS FALSIFYING TEST SCORES," and tales of the greed and misdeeds of business leaders, it's easy to be influenced by what you see or hear. Yet the reality is, most professional athletes don't take performance-enhancing drugs, most business leaders don't cheat, and most teachers are trustworthy. Don't extrapolate to your company or community.

❖ **Look for the good.** Dr. Rick Hanson, neuropsychologist and author of *Hardwiring Happiness* encourages "self-directed neuroplasticity"; that is, intentionally using your mind to change your brain. "The key," he says, "is a controlled use of attention. Attention is like a spotlight, to be sure, shining on things within our awareness. But it's also like a vacuum cleaner, sucking whatever it rests upon into the brain, for better or worse. For example, if we rest our attention routinely on what we resent or regret—our hassles, our lousy roommate, what Jean-Paul Sartre called 'hell' (other people)—then we're going to build out the neural substrates of those thoughts and feelings."[16] If you pay more attention to what people do right than wrong; operate with assumptions that people thrive when trusted, not when controlled; and actively look for the results of that, you'll begin to rewire how your brain thinks about trust.

The first mistake many make when trusting is believing that trust is an all-or-nothing proposition; in other words, "I either trust you or I don't." Trust is not a trust-yes, trust-no switch, and it's not unconditional. Authentic trust, the kind you need to build and sustain a thriving Trust, Inc., isn't a screensaver waiting in the background until it's needed. Rather, it's a process and learned skill. Trust building requires relationship building. It's ongoing. How to do that is a focus of Part II.

ASSESSING THE RISK

When my husband and I moved to Montana from the East Coast, we decided to build a house in a small community near Glacier National Park. We sought recommendations from our real estate agent, researched contractors, and met top contenders—we thought we had done our due diligence when we hired a personable local builder we both quickly trusted. Two years later he was in jail, and we had a half-finished house and thousands of dollars in unpaid bills to contractors and suppliers. That "trusted" builder had re-appropriated our funds for his personal use.

Now, with distance, it's easy to see how we got our trust-signals wrong. His engaging style created a halo effect, which we sought, and did confirm during the selection process. We used confirmation bias to affirm what we already believed—he was, indeed, a builder we could trust. It was an expensive lesson, both emotionally and financially.

I'm a strong advocate for trusting others, and a stronger one for challenging beliefs, assessing risk, and honing one's trust-giving skills. There's risk if you trust and find that trust betrayed, but there's also risk if you don't trust, because that distrust fuels disengagement and unwanted behaviors, reduces well-being, and diminishes results. Neither scenario is what you want. Because you're the only person who can assess your personal risk in a given situation and how comfortable you are with trusting someone, my intention is to offer you "when in doubt" considerations. The trick is not to tune out or ignore doubts, but to use them to spark thinking. Trusting others involves thoughtful consideration and judgment.

How do you decide to trust or not trust? This checklist of considerations is intended as a guide for thinking through the dilemma. When in doubt, ask yourself:

Checklist: Assessing Your Trust-Risk
✓ How important is this task/issue/project? What's at stake for me if it fails or if something goes wrong? What's at stake for the other person?

✓ What checks and balances or safety nets are currently in place to mitigate my risk? If there aren't any, what can I establish to limit risk and increase my sense of security?

✓ What's the worst thing that can happen if I give this person my trust, related to this issue?

✓ What's the best thing that can happen if I give this person my trust, related to this issue?

✓ What boundaries can I create, while still offering freedom within, that will contain the risk?

✓ Even if I make a decision to trust this person, related to this issue, how can I revisit how it's going, without micro-managing or impacting his or her perceived sense of trust?

✓ What issue(s) am I struggling with related to trusting him or her: ability, character, past experience, limited experience, communication style, performance level, dissimilar values, or importance of situation? Do those reservations affect the outcome or just cloud my decision?

✓ Does trusting him or her increase my vulnerability or impact future interactions?

✓ What level of trust could I give as a first step?

✓ Will this relationship be impacted if I don't offer trust to this person in this situation? How? Why?

Some people are more risk-avoidant or risk-tolerant than others based on their life-experience factors, which impact how they approach everything from relationships to money. Understanding your own experiences with trust can help you gain insight into potential resistance or over-trusting. Even power-level or status can influence whether you trust others or not. Researchers from Ohio State University's Fisher College of Business found, "high-status people tend to trust people more in initial encounters than did people with lower status." The lead author of that study, Professor Robert Lount, noted, "People have high status because other people like and admire them. The result is that high-status individuals come to expect that others are going to treat them well, which make them more likely to trust."[17]

THE TRUST, INC. REALITY

You can't create trust currency to fuel your Trust, Inc. without giving trust. You can't operate a winning culture without trusting others. And you can't reap the dividends of igniting passions, engagement, and innovation unless you trust.

Even small amounts of trust signal the desire for developing a trusting relationship in time. That's an important concept for any manager. Certainly people aren't trustworthy to the same level, but when you choose to offer your trust incrementally and situationally, you increase the likelihood of reaping the dividends produced by growing trust currency.

Even through occasional untrustworthy bosses, peers, and staff experiences, personal mistakes in trust-giving, and a few serious trust betrayals, I can affirm the risk of trusting is exceeded by its benefits. You can't build genuine relationships with yourself or others without trust. Despite discouraging statistics and sound bites heralding the challenges of trust in an era of distrust, good news comes from science: Scientists at Emory University discovered that "choosing trust over cynicism, generosity over selfishness, makes the brain light up with quiet joy."[18]

CHAPTER 5

Enable Accountability and Innovation

It is not only what we do, but also what we do not do, for which we are accountable.

~ Moliere

This isn't a chapter on how to "hold others" accountable, set and manage goals, or accomplish classic supervisory or management-related tasks. It's not a chapter about the external elements of accountability found in compliance, or in standards-driven or regulation-required disclosures to eliminate legal risk—as if saying, "Hey, I told you." Nor is it a chapter concerned with the mandated account-giving approaches of many industries, institutions, companies, and leaders. Although all these elements have a place in instilling confidence in societal or organizational systems, in public and legal frameworks, and in consumer safety, external accountability is not a fuel for authentic trust. *Real* accountability is.

This chapter focuses on a keystone needed for creating and spending trust currency: *accountability as the ability to be counted on*. It addresses what happens to trust when you regularly demonstrate you can be counted on and when you don't. When you enable real accountability in your trust-pocket, you'll be rewarded with increasing staff accountability, exceptional results, and thriving innovation. You'll even enhance how others perceive your trustworthiness, despite occasional mistakes or errors in judgment. Here's the formula: *Trust, in the form of currency given, enables accountability and innovation.*

REAL ACCOUNTABILITY

Most people apply accountability to other people's results and actions. They want *others* to be *more* accountable. When trust is broken or things go wrong, they want to "hold someone accountable." This 21st-century equivalent of witch hunting comes with finger-pointing, blaming, pundits, tweets, blog ramblings, and public outcry.

When scandals fill headlines, battle cries for more accountability and transparency escalate. When stakeholder confidence is shattered, accountability becomes the repetitive buzzword. And when organizational goals fall short, results falter, or initiatives fail, the process to ferret out wrongdoers is not only proclaimed in the public square, but also propagated in rumor mills, halting voluntary collaboration, risk taking, and innovation.

People who operate with authentic trust at work understand accountability's role in trust-building. They *first* apply accountability to themselves. These Trust, Inc. leaders approach accountability from the vantage point of being *personally* accountable—the ownership of self.

Consider the emotional shift that would occur if you knew with certainty that you could count on your boss—*really* count on him to be in your corner, smooth the way, own up to issues, work in partnership, deliver on promises, authentically show up, and give you his trust. If you've ever worked for someone like that, you know it makes you feel safe to offer ideas, take thoughtful risks, and invest your passions and discretionary efforts toward a bigger purpose. His real accountability raises the bar of what you expect from yourself, and it changes how you work in return.

In the words of Linda Galindo, author of _The 85% Solution_, "True accountability is 'personal accountability' and the only way to achieve it is to take responsibility for the outcomes of your choices, behaviors and actions."[1] At its core, real accountability is about trust. When we own what we do, or what we don't do, and hold ourselves accountable for what occurs, good or not, we become people others can count on. For those who manage and lead in our workplaces, that "ability to be counted on" is foundational for staff confidence and trust, which in turn fuels innovation. Trust offers the risk-taking security that innovation requires.

Sounds great, right? But no surprise it's not easy to do. How do you hold yourself accountable? How do you evaluate the results and consequences your behaviors and decisions produce? How do others evaluate these same actions? And how does any of it impact a Trust, Inc. culture that enables accountability and innovation? Let's take a look.

The Unspoken Obligations of Trust

As the leader of your Trust, Inc., consider the unspoken obligations, the expectations, as it were, of those working in your trust-pocket. Whether you agree or disagree that these _should_ be their expectations, the reality is they are.

- **You're responsible for trust.** No, you're not responsible for everyone trusting everyone; you're responsible for being a trusted boss, trusting others, and operating with the five essentials to spark trust. You're also a catalyst for keeping your trust-culture alive (find tips on how in Chapter 11). Perspective about trust responsibility comes from authors

Solomon and Flores: "If we think of trust as something that is created and bestowed as part of a shared social practice instead of 'simply there' in a relationship or society, trust moves into the realm of responsibility."[2] I think of it as being responsible for investing trust.

- **There are trust consequences to your actions.** There is an ebb and flow of trust that accountability affects. When a staff member's poor performance is ignored and she's allowed to continue underperforming without consequences, when you drop the ball with a peer or boss on a promise made to your team, when you take the easy way out of a difficult situation instead of the right way, or when you turn a blind eye to negative behaviors from others, expect trust to wane. Expect it to grow when the opposite occurs. Real accountability is the *willing* ownership of decisions, actions, behaviors, and results. Real accountability is an unspoken obligation of authentic trust.

- **You operate with a "more beyond" perspective.** Spain, in the 15th century, considered itself the western point of civilization. In its coat of arms was the motto *ne plus ultra*, meaning "nothing more beyond." When Columbus made that obsolete, Queen Isabella removed the "ne" making the motto "more beyond." The same is true for Trust, Inc. leaders. There's more beyond. To get great results, your trust-pocket must align with your organization's vision, values, and/or mission, supporting its goals and objectives. That requires a big-team mindset and includes support and collaboration beyond your trust-pocket. When you can be counted on by your bosses, peers, customers, and coworkers, you create a smoother path for those you lead to get things done "beyond" your work group.

When You're Wrong

I once worked for a boss who was never wrong, never made a mistake or a bad decision, and suffered from selective amnesia. To his staff he was Teflon Man: Nothing stuck to him and everything came sliding toward us. Accountability was not a concept he practiced unless things turned out well, and then he claimed credit. But if they didn't, he embarked on endeavors to identify someone responsible. Being called to his office typically meant he was seeking information to decide whom to blame.

Justify. Justify. Justify. Like a battle cry, he commissioned reports, graphs, charts, and documentation whenever his boss questioned him. He found it easier to dig in his heels than to admit he might be wrong, or change his mind. Working for someone I couldn't respect eventually led me to transfer departments. But, it still baffles me. People do make mistakes, trip up, and, on occasion, speak or act in error. And while there's nothing that says we should be happy about it when we do it ourselves, trying to act as though it didn't happen, covering mistakes, or justifying inaccurate positions leads nowhere and decreases the likelihood that those you lead will count on you.

Unlike that early boss of mine, people with a thriving Trust, Inc. speak up and admit mistakes. They take accountability for fixing the resulting problems. And even if they have to gather their courage and swallow hard, they acknowledge when they're wrong.

In 20 years in management I learned that playing it safe, isn't. If you want to create trust currency, one of the biggest mistakes you can make is pointing fingers, blaming others, or offering excuses. Own your decisions, choices, and actions. Admit when you're wrong. Fix your mistakes. Then learn from them and move on. These are the signs of confident, accountable, initiative-filled people. If you behave that way, others will too.

There's a story often attributed to famed British economist John Maynard Keynes, about being confronted by a man after a lecture. The man insisted Keynes give him an explanation of why he contradicted himself with something written years before. "Well," Keynes replied. "When I'm wrong, I change my mind." Seems to me that's good advice for leaders too. Despite media pundits who pounce on a politician's "flip-flop," implying that everyone should remain in cement-grounded positions regardless of personal growth, learning, and societal changes, changing your mind when you're wrong is strength, not weakness.

Owning mistakes shows strength too. When a Nordstrom sales associate in another state failed to send other purchased items with the altered outfit I needed for an important conference, I heard from her before the package even arrived. She called to tell me it was her fault and she was terribly sorry. Not only did her call help me plan replacement items for that business trip, but it also increased my goodwill toward her and Nordstrom.

Acknowledging mistakes is viewed positively, even in unexpected industries. It used to be that hospitals and doctors were reluctant to admit errors for fear of lawsuits. That's changing. A spokesman for The Sorry Works! Coalition notes, "Apologies for medical errors, along with upfront compensation, reduces anger of patients and families, which leads to a reduction in medical malpractice lawsuits and associated litigation."[3]

When people are sincere and demonstrate real accountability that acknowledges they too are human and make mistakes, it builds, not diminishes, trust. Mark Twain's advice works—"When in doubt, tell the truth."

REFLECTIVE THINKING
Are You Holding Yourself Accountable?

Consider these questions. Insights are more likely if you write your answers.

1. When was the last time you said you were sorry for a poor decision you made that impacted your staff? If you've rarely or never apologized to staff, consider why. If you do when needed, what benefit do you find from it?

2. Think of a time when you had to face your boss or other senior leaders and "own up" to a big error. What can you learn from that experience (plus or minus) that helps you create a culture in which ownership and correction of mistakes is reinforced?

3. Make a mental note the next time you find yourself "digging in" to defend or refute a decision or position that was not optimal. Ask yourself why you are doing this? Are you afraid to change your mind? What are you gaining (or losing) by standing firm?

THE SPIRIT, NOT THE LETTER

Avoiding wrongdoing is not the same as doing right. There's a difference between something legal and something ethical; something in compliance and something fair; something one turns a blind eye to and something one is compelled to address. As 20th-century Supreme Court Justice Potter Stewart remarked, "Ethics is knowing the difference between what you have a right to do and what is right to do."

Those who operate with a rules-based approach delineating what can and can't be done as an attempt to "legislate" morality and ethics miss the deeper connection to trust and accountability. It's not what you technically *can* do that matters to those you lead, it's what you *should* do—what's right to do. People see other's actions as a reflection of their character, beliefs, and values.

The executive who flew from her New York office to Chicago to personally inform staff about their branch closing demonstrated a depth of character and valuing others that's memorable, not just for those affected but also those unscathed in other branches. What comes to mind about a director's values when, unable to give raises to staff for two years, he negotiated away his own bonus, asking it to be divided among his team?

We don't hear about people such as these as often as we hear about those who e-mailed the layoff message or cut everyone's salary but their own. The reality is, both exist and both have impact. Their actions, just as do yours, have consequences—positive and negative. One thing is certain: How people judge your character by your actions gets assimilated into your culture. Some call it "shadow of the leader." Actions speak. What do yours say?

Check Yourself Tips

❖ **YouTube reality check.** If what you're about to do becomes public, say, via a video on YouTube, would you be proud of it? Would anything your coworkers see or hear as a result of your actions cause them to withdraw trust?

❖ **Mother-watching check.** If your mom knew what decision you were going to make or what you were doing, would she approve? Would she do it?

❖ **Other people check.** If others made the same decision you're planning to implement, would you be okay with it? Would it be fine if *everyone* did this?

❖ **Outside the room check.** If you walked out of the room and had to abide by the decision you made, would you still make it?

We elevate others' behavior when we elevate our own. Research confirms "ethical leaders can influence followers to behave ethically."[4] Unfortunately, the reverse is true. Real accountability heightens behavior. Coming from the inside, this intrinsic element creates "felt responsibility," or the degree to which we "feel personally accountable and responsible for the results of the work" we do.[5] That contrasts with extrinsic accountability, or the external monitoring or controls that others place on us, used to "hold people accountable," and encourage disclosure or reporting. However, whereas extrinsic accountability can be necessary, external systems of accountability won't get you a Trust, Inc. culture enabling real accountability and innovation.

The workplace has changed. As I wrote in *The Titleless Leader*, "those who lead in the business world won't get followers just because their title says they should. Employees decide to whom they'll give their ideas, enthusiasm, and commitment."[6] Author Dov Seidman puts it well: "Leadership is no longer about formal authority that commands and controls and exerts power *over* people, but rather about moral authority that connects and collaborates and generates power *through* people."[7]

A Sense of Fairness

One essential component to "moral authority," and the ability to enable accountability and innovation using trust currency, is the issue of fairness. People care about both outcome and process. However, researchers W. Chan Kim and Renee Mauborgne found that process matters more: "Their central finding is that employees will commit to a manager's decision—even one they disagree with— if they believe that the process the manager used to make the decision was fair."[8]

Fair systems involve asking for input and engaging people in the process, explaining how final decisions are made, and ensuring understanding about its impacts on expectations or "new rules of the game." Fairness is not about consensus, harmony, agreement, compromise, or support. It's about involvement, transparency, and clarity. In the following exercise, consider how you might perceive the actions given in the examples if you worked in those environments.

REFLECTIVE EXERCISE
Fair or Not Fair?

Circle the decision-making processes you think would result in greater trust.

TRUST, INC.

1. A group of supervisors spend two days off site working on a new Internet access policy. The following week, each supervisor provides her staff with a memo detailing the changes.

2. Five staff members are selected by their manager to meet with productivity consultants who will be redesigning internal systems. Two months later, changes are rolled out.

3. Staff members are randomly selected to provide software engineers their "wishlist" of changes needed in the department's applications. A composite of that information is presented to the entire staff for discussion prior to the manager's final decision.

4. HR announces a new compensation system they've been working on for a year. Each supervisor was sent a package of information to discuss with individuals who will receive a salary adjustment based on the policy change.

5. Budgets are tight and cuts will be made. Each location director is asked to submit suggestions and revenue-saving ideas in consultation with staff. As part of implementation, employee forums are held to discuss the why and what, and how decided cuts will affect each area.

Self-scoring: Numbers three and five offer the best chance for creating a sense of fairness and trust.

Not every decision requires staff involvement. However, many managers still believe questioning challenges authority, *fair* means equal, input necessitates consensus, and withholding information increases power. But those who operate with trust currency realize all good ideas are not in one head, and an engaged staff means better results. They operate their winning culture with a winning philosophy: It's only when we're all winning that we all win.

THE TRUST–ACCOUNTABILITY CONNECTION

Work doesn't happen in isolation. To whom are you accountable, and for what? Staff. Bosses. Peers. Customers. Supporters. Volunteers. Members. Suppliers. Investors. Community. It's often a long and growing list depending on role, organization, and industry. You have numerous individual trust–accountability opportunities and connections.

For this example, let's look at a common connection—our boss. If I'm your boss, I may or may not entrust you with resources, budgets, results, and decision making. I may or may not invest my trust in your actions, or feel comfortable with the risk. Your role is to enable the growth of my trust currency once I invest *even a little* in you. My role is to go first, to start trust by giving you trust (see Chapter 6). You'll increase the odds I'll take that first step, then a second and third, if you operate with personal, i.e. *real* accountability. It works the same way with your staff.

Trust-Accountability Circles

You start the accountabilty circle by giving trust

Staff offers accountabilitiy in return

Even a little trust sparks the opportunity for accountability; then accountability enables more trust. This simple exchange triggers the beginning of an accountability circle.

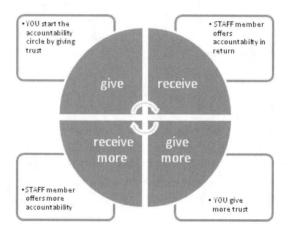

When you give trust, and your staff returns accountability, their action facilitates the making of trust currency and triggers more trust-giving. That enables an accountability circle to grow with time. As trust currency is created by this exchange, what the relationship "looks like" changes too. Once trust currency exists, you and your staff have a medium of exchange for what you each want. You might offer, or a staff member might want greater responsibility, more interesting work, additional resources, or flexibility. Your relationship grows or shrinks based on the trust–accountability connection. Without accountability returned, the trust that's given isn't fueled.

Accountability circles vary in size and scope in each relationship. Central to this trust–accountability connection is an understanding that accountability builds trust currency. In fact, authentic trust requires it. Being counted on—in other words, real accountability—increases trust because it's grounded in actions demonstrating a mutual commitment to the relationship. However, accountability doesn't start trust. *You start trust by giving it.*

THE TRUST—INNOVATION CONNECTION

"Practically every individual...possesses unique information that can be put to use only with 'his active cooperation.' Getting that cooperation may well turn out to be one of the key managerial issues of the next few decades," according to Friedrich Hayek, a Nobel laureate economist.[9] That's the essence of the trust—innovation connection: Ideas can't be crowbarred from heads; they must be willingly given. And they're only given to those we trust. Consider these research findings:

- "Organizational trust is one of the key factors in the creation of a social environment in which ideas are freely generated, honestly assessed and selected, and collectively transformed into profitable new products and services."[10]

- "Employees' trust in their immediate supervisor is positively related to organizational innovativeness."[11]

- "Employees who experience a high-trust environment are 22 times more likely to be willing to take risks that could benefit the company."[12]

Work is speeding up. Trust increases your team's ability to make things happen faster, better, easier. It reduces the friction that stalls projects and dismantles idea-sharing. It increases the satisfaction of contribution and the excitement of turning ideas into reality. Building trust is not a nice thing to do; it's a strategic one. You can use trust to enable innovation at your Trust, Inc., with:

- ❖ **A safe environment for risk-taking.** The linguistic root of *trust* comes from the old Norse word *traust*, meaning, "a feeling of security."[13] That's exactly what innovation requires. Ideas don't emerge or evolve in workplaces filled with fear, dark-side politics, ill intentions, or controlling leaders. For people to volunteer thoughts and ideas, or engage in the process of turning others' ideas into solutions, they need an environment conducive to sharing, collaboration, open communication, honesty, and integrity. That's the environment trust builds.

❖ **An openness to ideas.** Not all companies, organizations, or trust-pockets are open to ideas, innovation, or evolution. They can still operate with trust, but some agencies, organizations, or industries are more change-averse than others. Some people are too, but an openness to ideas can be cultivated with time. In your trust-pocket, openness starts with you. Listen to what you say when others push to change things you think don't need changing. As Marianne Williamson reminds us, "The world changes when we change."

❖ **A suspension of judgment.** You need to evaluate and make decisions as part of a leadership role, but when it comes to innovation, that skill can block you. The challenge is learning to turn off the judging, evaluating, and assessing you've trained yourself to be good at, and help teammates do the same. Reframe thinking from *why-this-won't-work* to *why-not-try-it?* Make Trust, Inc. a place where people try and fail, test and change, create and re-create, practice and learn, and green-house and nurture their own and others' ideas. As Einstein said, "We can't solve problems by using the same kind of thinking we used when we created them."

YOUR ACTIONS RIPPLE

Real accountability goes beyond being counted on for what and how we do something. It involves a deeper commitment to best-of-self behaviors—being answerable for the person we are, how we "show up," and whether we add to or subtract from the world we share. It's ownership of self, at its deepest level.

Our actions ripple. Sometimes they create lasting impact, inspire others, or ignite positive reactions. Sometimes it's the opposite. In either case, we're accountable. How we see ourselves "in action," or how we don't, impacts our ability to practice *real* accountability.

What I witnessed on the way home from a long trip provides an example. In rumpled, second-day clothes after a canceled flight, my husband and I finally arrived at our community airport, anxious to collect luggage and get home to a shower. Instead, we found ourselves waiting to report missing luggage.

I couldn't help overhearing the conversation between a father and his college-aged daughter behind us. She was joining her family for a week's snowboarding vacation and her overstuffed snowboard bag had arrived, but her suitcase hadn't. She'd left that morning from the East Coast and her missing bag contained what she planned to wear that evening. She was whining about her inconvenience. But it was her father who changed the tone for the worse. As he reminisced with his daughter about past travel mishaps, it became clear this dad was used to escalating his outrage until he got what he wanted, unaware of how his actions impact others. Ranting about the inefficiencies of small-town airports and incompetent staffs, his venomous words fueled their plan: "Maybe you should do what you did in St. Thomas," she suggested, offering to start the process by demonstrating her dismay to the agent first. "I can cry if you want," she offered. "No," he said. "Let me handle it. I'm in the mood to let someone have it and get you a free ticket or vouchers."

It wasn't their frustration over displaced baggage that startled me; it was the way they chose to *be*; how he had taught his daughter to be. Lacking accountability for the way they "showed up," their actions rippled with toxic emotions and increased an already harried agent's stress.

Earlier that afternoon, while catching up on e-mail, I'd read a daily meditation about actions. *All things are important—they all count*, it reminded. It's true. Actions. Behaviors. Words. Who you are. What you do. How you show up. It matters. We're accountable for the ripples we leave. Those who build trust, inspire great work, and create mutually beneficial relationships shape a positive future with their ripples.

PART II

AT TRUST, INC., YOU SPARK
TRUST WITH FIVE ESSENTIALS

Every man's work, whether it be literature or music or pictures or architecture or anything else, is always a portrait of himself.

~ Samuel Butler

CHAPTER 6

Go First

The best way to find out if you can trust somebody is to trust them.
~ Ernest Hemingway

We don't trust the people who work for us very much. At least that's the impression many employers give. Consider the hiring process: Whole industries thrive on pre-employment assessments to ensure honesty, integrity, and attitudinal match. Then, they offer protection from a multitude of problems an untrustworthy staff might create. There are armbands to measure productivity, watchful cameras, biometric time clocks, monitoring software, blocked Websites, ethics training, carrot-and-stick programs, and even apps that can spy on staff.

Articles abound reinforcing the "don't trust staff" position— "You're Their Boss, Not Their Babysitter"; "Ten Ways to Spy on Your

Staff"; "How to Supervise Bad Attitudes and Negative Behaviors." By contrast, few headlines proclaim "Innovative Employees Save Company," or "How Leaders Can Get out of the Way and Let Exceptional Work Happen," or "Why Top Leaders Trust Employees."

The unspoken truth, or its perception, is that collectively as bosses we don't trust employees to be responsible adults, manage their talents and aspirations, or be self-motivated to do great work. We don't trust them to use good judgment, make difficult decisions, or improve our business—at least, not without our directives, rules, or leadership.

These are the same employees who write novels at night, run community charities, parent children, create apps, manage households, take night classes, handle difficult life issues, and develop ideas and businesses in their spare time. These are the same people who volunteer in disasters, help out neighbors, and quietly support or care for family members. Do we think coming to work changes their character?

Douglas McGregor's management classic, *The Human Side of Enterprise*, published in 1960, made "Theory X and Theory Y" leadership concepts popular. Theory Y leaders believe that, in general, people want to do a good job, and will, given the right environment. By contrast, Theory X leaders believe people are unproductive and unreliable, and the only way to get results from them is to prod, threaten, and control.[1] Five decades later, these differing roots about the inherent nature of people and how to manage them continue to influence workplace policies, procedures, and the way those who lead view those who don't.

What's the norm where you work—Theory X or Theory Y leader beliefs? In one of my workshops a Theory X leader commented, "I decided a long time ago to expect *nothing* from my staff," she said. "That way, I'll never be disappointed." It was clear she wasn't. If you expect that employees can't be trusted, and are slackers out to take advantage of well-meaning leaders, you'll find it. If you expect the opposite, you'll find that. Your thinking impacts not only what you notice, but also what you influence. Acting in accordance with your expectations enables those expectations to become true. What do you expect? Theory X behaviors or Theory Y? Whichever it is for you, it will affect how you view the information in this chapter.

This chapter begins Part II of the book, addressing how to spark trust with five essentials:

1. **Go first.**
2. **Elevate your communication.**
3. **Demonstrate behavioral integrity.**
4. **Show up authentically.**
5. **Build genuine relationships.**

We can acquire "knowing" related to trust's organizational impact—from passionate staffs and exceptional results to high engagement and innovation. But without putting it into everyday practice—the "doing" behind the desired outcome—nothing ignites, happens, or changes. Information doesn't change or build results and trusted relationships, *you* do.

This is a pivotal chapter. It hinges on a simple concept: If you can't, or won't, trust the people who work for you, there can be no thriving Trust, Inc. Operating with trust as a verb is an evolving process for most leaders.

Still, the reality is this: You won't spark trust, won't create sustainable trust currency, won't enable a business culture where people do great work, unless you go first and give trust. If you struggle with that concept or question how you can "go first," if you hold that others must "earn your trust," I hope you find in these pages insights and perspectives enabling you to open a mental door, even a tiny one, to that possibility. As you explore this chapter and those that follow, I hope you'll consider Emily Dickinson's words and "Dwell in possibility."

OPENING THE DOOR OF POSSIBILITY

Not far from the magical-looking gumdrop mountains along the Li River in China, just outside of Guilin, we visited the Reed Flute Cave. I find caves intimidating—perhaps it's the darkness, apprehension of the unknown, or my active imagining of lurking critters, but they're not typically an experience I seek. The caves or caverns I've visited I can count on one hand.

This cave excursion was an extra for the educational tour group I was traveling with, and I decided to go along. At the entrance, I hesitated. If it hadn't been for a nudge from my husband, I'd have changed my mind. But similar to my other cave experiences, my concerns were unwarranted. I was richly rewarded with a world of wonder and amazement, realizing early in the walk with a local guide that I should never have doubted what awaited would be worth pushing past the trepidation.

Stepping into the world of authentic trust-giving can feel like my cave experience—a little overwhelming, concerning, or threatening at times. But authentic trust offers unimagined wonders too. It opens pathways to mutually beneficial relationships. By its very nature, being *in genuine relationship with* someone changes both you and the other person.

A door of possibility opens when a trusting relationship begins. What can you now accomplish, as trust evolves, that you wouldn't have been able to do without it? What new connections, insights, ideas, or opportunities will come to you or them as a result? How will the relationship enhance your understanding, learning, or growth, or those of the other person? What you're able to achieve with trusted others is vastly different from what you can do alone.

A wonderful world awaits. It's not a world of stalactites, stalagmites, and rock formations, but passion, engagement, and innovation; a world of personal depth, brightness, and possibility. Here are a few of the sights you may encounter:

What Authentic Trust Can Render	
Deep and genuine relationships	Speed, enthusiasm, energy, and fun
Self-awareness and personal growth	Commitment, motivation, involvement
Well-being and enhanced optimism	Individual and collective achievement
Application of gifts and talents	Transformational interconnection
Collective intelligence and its fruits	Reciprocity; being needed and "seen"
New ideas, methods, solutions	Confidence in self and others
Elevated communication	Integrity, ethics, doing what's right
Authenticity and self-alignment	Engaged being and personal insights
Safe harbor for innovation and risk-taking	Winning philosophies; big-team thinking
Beyond self; influence of the collective	Renewed purpose; making a difference
Self-governing and accountability	Positive, productive environment

Enhanced thinking and understanding	A sense of purpose and contribution
Breakthroughs in thinking	Productive problem-solving
Mutual benefit, support, and reliance	Great work; great results

Similar to the wonders inside the earth, those that evolve from authentic trust grow slowly throughout time. Work and business relationships are complex. So is authentic trust. Not because, as an emotional skill, authentic trust is difficult to understand or do. It's not. But it gets confused with other kinds of trust. So much so that "Scholars continue to express concern regarding their collective lack of consensus about trust's meaning."[2]

As economist and professor Oliver Williamson wrote, "...trust is a term with many meanings." The word is used regularly to describe how you feel about everything from your car (you trust it) to your boss (you don't). Fortunately, the trust needed for a thriving culture is one kind: authentic. Here's the definition for this book, in case you missed it in the Introduction:

authentic trust \ *verb.* \ **1.** Trust(ing), as in committing to, giving, or placing confidence in another, with awareness and optimism. **2.** Choosing actions associated with genuine relationship-creating, -building, -restoring; requires ongoing cultivation. **3.** A dynamic happening *in* relationships, created and grown only when there is an ongoing commitment to the relationship, and when that relationship is more important than any single outcome. Accepts risk of trust-betrayed. **4.** Given without concern for personal advantage, enabling others to show up with talents and do great work. **5.** Requires self-awareness; a relationship practice with self that offers ways to explore individual gifts, possibilities, and potential.

MISUNDERSTOOD TRUTHS ABOUT AUTHENTIC TRUST

Only when there is a commitment to the relationship is authentic trust possible. When mutual commitments are delivered without concern for personal advantage, and without attempted manipulation or control, authentic trust grows. Consider these misunderstood truths about authentic trust[3]—the trust essential for your Trust, Inc.:

- **Trust isn't always a good thing.** Trust isn't good or bad. It's how, when, why, and to whom it's given that determines its positive or negative impact. There are many types of trust. Non-authentic, simple trust, can be unrealistic, naïve, foolish, or blind. Yet, many still operate with only simple trust, the kind we developed as children. Authentic trust is sophisticated and questioning—it's open-eyes trust.

- **Distrust isn't the opposite of trust.** Control is. Notice where there's a lack of authentic trust and you'll find controlling people, tight reins, micromanaging, and fear that trusting brings unacceptable risk. When authentic trust is given with good judgment, incrementally, it fuels and is fueled by accountability. Authentic trust is not stagnant, but a dynamic, growing or shrinking entity, affecting the generation of trust currency—the medium of exchange in the new workplace.

- **There's always risk when giving trust.** Giving trust is a developed skill requiring critical thought and experience. It doesn't deny the past, or ignore a possibility of broken trust, either intentional or unintentional. Those operating with authentic trust evaluate risks and benefits before giving it. Once given, authentic trust shouldn't be taken for granted, especially in a changing landscape. It requires ongoing management, scrutiny, nurturing, and judgment.

- **Trust is a process.** Authentic trust is not a screensaver waiting in the background until it's needed; it's not strong glue holding everything together. As a learned skill, it's a way of operating involving choice and action. Authentic trust enables relationship-creating, -building, -restoring, and -nurturing. It's not something you own or have; it's something you do, requiring commitment, ongoing effort, and reciprocity. When the relationship is more important than any one outcome, the process of authentic trust-building is possible.

- **Trust is about people, not things.** Trust involves interpersonal engagement. We may use the word and associate *trust* with things as well as people, but one can't really "trust" their car. We confuse *trust* with *dependable* or *reliable*. Authentic trust requires commitments made and commitments honored. It necessitates decision, action, and response. Authentic trust, at its core, is relationship or interpersonal trust.

- **Trust is conditional and situational.** There are limits and conditions with authentic trust. When you say you trust someone, there's a presumed conditionality. For example, I may trust my mechanic to work on my car, but I don't trust him to do a root canal. I may trust you to handle this problem in *this* situation, but not in *every* situation. Whereas unconditional love is a positive, unconditional trust isn't. Unconditional trust implies blind or naïve trust. Authentic trust has conditions, boundaries, and limits. One condition is competence. People need to be able to do, or be capable of doing, what you need them to do, before authentic trust is given. My 4-year-old granddaughter can mix up brownies, but no amount of trust enables her to stuff and bake a turkey.

- **To get trust you must give it.** Nineteenth-century English novelist Charlotte Yonge wrote, "The mistake we make is when we seek to be beloved, instead of loving." The same is true of trust. The mistake leaders make is seeking only to be trusted, instead of trusting. If you want to be a trusted boss, you must go first—you must give trust. You may be loveable, but that won't get you love—only loving will. Sharing, not hoarding information gets you communication, and re-spect comes by respecting others. As a relationship process, authentic trust is no different. Contrary to popular belief, trust, like love, is not earned. You start trust by giving trust. Learning *how* to trust is more of a challenge than deciding whom to trust.

- **Authentic trust brings good news.** Unlike simple trust, which can't be rebuilt once broken, authentic trust can. That's good news for employers and employees reeling from broken trust during the Great Recession, for Trust, Inc. leaders recognizing they make unintentional mistakes that diminish trust, and for anyone desiring to restore well-being and trusting relationships. If a work relationship matters, there's the possibility for trust to be restored in time. (More about how in Chapter 11.)

Authentic trust, like love, is cultivated, grown, and nurtured. We spark authentic trust by going first. We make it by what we do and how we do it; by what we say and how we say it; by showing up and being authentic; and by giving it away.

HOW TO GIVE TRUST AWAY

I'm with 20th-century humorist Will Rogers, who said, "I would rather be the man who bought the Brooklyn Bridge than the man who sold it." No one wants to hire a con man, risk failed results, or believe in false promises. And we don't want to risk our careers, reputation, or professional clout by being naïve about giving trust at work. However, many bosses do the equivalent without realizing it, operating with the functional equivalent of "I trust you" or "I don't trust you." They view trust as an all-or-nothing approach—the equivalent of an on-off switch. Their trust or lack of trust is unmiti-gated, unconditional, and unqualified. It's also naïve.

In my first management role, I operated with that simple, naïve kind of trust, believing I could either trust someone or I couldn't. That black-or-white thinking meant those I managed either lived up to my trust standard or didn't. It also meant my work group achieved only mediocre results.

Once I learned how authentic trust could transform work relationships and cultures, my self-awareness, leadership skills, and results soared. Throughout the years, I've become an advocate for authentic trust-building, watching its power transform dysfunctional work-teams into thriving trust-pockets—transforming businesses, impacting leaders, and sparking the kind of staff innovation, engagement, and passion missing in most workplaces. Following are a few basics I learned along the way.

Step One Basics: Trust-Giving Tips

❖ **Give early and simply.** In a new work relationship, quickly give a little trust as soon as you have a chance. A little trust transmits a desire to build a relationship. Help create a successful outcome and your intention is clear. For example, Emily joins your team and you invite her to sit in on an important meeting with a peer. A few issues in her area of expertise require researching, so you ask Emily which she'd like to work on, offering assistance if she has questions, and pointing her in the right direction. By inviting her to the meeting and providing her an opportunity to report back at the next one, you gave a little trust, didn't micro-manage, and provided her with a safety net as a new employee.

❖ **Give individually.** People's skills, knowledge, and experience are different, so the incremental trust given to staff members will vary. Emily, who's inexperienced and new, *might* require trust-giving different from Jason, a knowledgeable person who's worked on the team. It's individual and situational. Time spent in a role doesn't necessarily equate to trust given. You might trust both Jason and Emily to lead a project team with little input, but only one to represent the company at a users meeting.

❖ **Give often.** Giving trust builds self-esteem and confidence, spurring engagement, commitment, and involvement. The more you give trust, the more you instill confidence. And when others in the work group see you regularly giving trust to coworkers, it establishes you as a trust-giver, not a trust-withholder. It assists people in seeing "what it looks like" to operate with trust currency in Trust, Inc. Trust begets trust. The more you give, the more you get.

THE EASY WAY TO GO FIRST

In my years of talking about authentic trust and helping people create trust-pockets, I started using an analogy about light switches and dimmer switches. The concept is simple: Think of authentic trust not as a light switch but a dimmer switch.[4] Going first by giving trust is like turning up a dimmer switch. Gradually, turn the light up to fit your needs. If it's too bright, turn it down; too low, turn it up. Giving trust is like that. It starts slowly, gradually, gently.

Central to a dimmer-switch model is the understanding discussed in the previous chapter that trust sparks the opportunity for accountability, which in turn enables more trust-giving.

Step Two Basics: Like Turning up a Dimmer Switch

❖ **Low—Run it by me first.** You can eliminate most trust-giving risk by using a dimmer-switch approach for trust-giving. Let's say there's a new person on your staff, or a seasoned person assigned an entirely new challenge. Give a little trust by starting on low. If the person runs it by you as requested, turn it up; give a little more trust according to risk, experience, communication level, and the person's unprompted accountability.

❖ **Medium—Keep me posted.** If you're comfortable with the trust level and find accountability demonstrated by the other person, adjust up, perhaps asking for regular updates. If meetings, reports, or updates turn up without prompting, you can move the trust level up a bit more.

❖ **High—Heads up if there's trouble.** Even at high trust levels, regular communication is essential to keep parties connected and current. High-trust work relationships operate on the get-into-trouble or need-my-help standard. That is, if it's working well you can expect a heads-up before a blow-up. Trust is adjusted upward as results, communication, and accountability levels prosper.

❖ **Too bright—Adjust back.** Trust fluctuates. If someone's performance or accountability has diminished, or results flounder, adjust the amount of trust given. Relationships built on authentic trust understand trust levels fluctuate based on work issues. Sometimes business issues, not personal performance, necessitate a trust level shift, such as with reorganizations, accelerated deadlines, and new bosses or initiatives.

Not every work situation facilitates an easy go-first, dimmer-switch incremental approach, and Chapter 11 will address other realities. You may also find it helpful to review the trust-risk questions in Chapter 4.

Although there are different ways to think about giving authentic trust first and to whom, I personally find it useful to revisit one question: Does the relationship or the outcome matter most in this situation? When you give trust first you are signaling that you're making an investment in the relationship. What signals do you typically give?

REFLECTIVE EXERCISE
Giving Trust First

Consider work relationships. Circle the statements that are more true than false for you, on average.

1. If someone gives me his or her trust, I'll give a little trust in return.

2. I think it's important to provide opportunities for people to demonstrate trustworthiness.

3. Basically, I think people should be trusted until proven otherwise.

4. People must first earn my trust.

5. I believe most people are inherently hard-working and honest.

6. I use good judgment before giving trust by assessing the risks associated with it.

7. I think most people at work are out for themselves.

8. As far as the people I work with, there are more reasons to trust than not trust.

9. As a boss, I'm responsible for taking the first steps toward building trusted relationships.

10. I invest in building strong relationships by giving incremental trust over time.

Self-scoring: Give yourself a point if you circled as true: 1, 2, 3, 5, 6, 8, 9, and 10. Multiply the result by 10. That number represents the probability that, today, you'd give trust first and by doing so signal you're investing in the relationship.

There are reasons why we trust people and reasons why we don't. That will always be the case. However, as you operate with authentic trust as a verb—the process of trusting, the making of trust currency, and the doing of actions that build relationships—it will enhance your understanding about who is worthy of your trust investment.

IF YOU BELIEVE PEOPLE MUST EARN YOUR TRUST

There's nothing I can write, no research studies I can cite, nor examples I can give that would be *enough* if you believe people must earn your trust. Only you can decide what that means, and how someone can "earn" your trust.

If you go to a dentist with a toothache, do you wait for her to earn your trust before she proceeds? If a trusted peer says he trusts a colleague, is that enough for you, or will that colleague need to earn your trust directly? How does a staff member earn trust if she's never given an opportunity to demonstrate she's trustworthy? And if she is given an opportunity, isn't that giving her a bit of trust? When is someone "good enough" to get trust from you? You're the only person who knows.

When we believe what we think—that people can't or can be trusted—our actions reflect our beliefs, even if there's information to the contrary. Being worthy of someone's trust and being trusted is not cause and effect. Someone being dependable, reliable, or counted on may increase the odds you'll think he or she is trustworthy, it doesn't correlate to you giving him or her your trust.

For example, if you work for a Theory X boss, who believes people are inherently not trustworthy, always self-serving, and looking out for themselves, no matter how trustworthy you are, it's unlikely you'll ever earn that person's trust. If, on the other hand, you work for a Theory Y boss, who believes people are inherently worthy of trust and often uses an on-off approach to basic trust, you'll be "trusted" generically, but not authentically.

You don't need trust given to you in order to be trustworthy. Likewise, being trustworthy doesn't ensure you'll receive trust—just as being loveable doesn't mean you'll always be loved. Some give trust to people who haven't demonstrated trustworthiness, hoping through time to help them learn about trust, or hoping to grow trust between them—just as people give love to people who haven't known love or aren't loving in return.

People can't earn authentic trust. By its very nature, authentic trust is given, created, and made. This may seem like semantics, but it's not. When you operate with trust as a verb, understanding it could be betrayed, but still giving it first, it communicates that you're investing in the other person and the relationship with a sense of optimism about the future.

By withholding trust until you decide someone has proven he's worthy of trust, or has "earned it," you communicate the opposite. Authentic trust requires a commitment; it's about the creating, building, restoring, and cultivating of genuine relationships. There are lots of kinds of trust. If someone needs to earn yours, consider the likelihood it's not the authentic trust you'll need to build a Trust, Inc.

INVESTING IN THE FUTURE— WHEN YOU GO FIRST

A significant trust occurrence happened for me in junior high. It started when my 8th-grade social studies teacher, Mr. Jones, asked me to stay after school. Already intimidated by him, as a shy and introverted student, I agonized the next two periods over having to talk to him.

What a surprise when I received his investment of trust. As the yearbook advisor, he asked me if I'd be the yearbook editor for the upcoming year. One might think he gave me the opportunity because I was a good student and he had confidence I could do the job. However, the reality was that although I was an A student in his class, the editor role involved tasks way outside my comfort zone. As a student who never raised her hand or participated in class unless prompted, he was "trusting" that I could cultivate the faculty relationships I'd need, lead a staff of 10 peer volunteers, and ask for help or support as needed.

Being trusted changed my confidence, self-awareness, and aspirations. Not instantly, of course, but as a result of that project's developmental challenges for me, and with Mr. Jones's increasing trust throughout the next year, I saw myself differently after that.

When you go first with authentic trust, that's what you do: You signal a positive intention. When you invest a bit of yourself in the success of another by giving your trust, you plant possibility seeds.

There's a favorite quote of mine from poet Edward Estlin Cummings, known as e.e. cummings, that captures the spark you're igniting when you give authentic trust: "We do not believe in ourselves until someone reveals that deep inside us something is valuable, worth listening to, worthy of our trust, sacred to our touch. Once we believe in ourselves we can risk curiosity, wonder, spontaneous delight or any experience that reveals the human spirit."[5]

You have great power to change lives, to make your work culture a place where people want to share their talents and gifts, and to spark new thinking, problem-solving, and possibilities. If you want to make that kind of difference at work, the first essential is simply: *go first.*

CHAPTER 7

Elevate Your Communication

The single biggest problem in communication is the illusion that it has taken place.

~ George Bernard Shaw

The cyclical, ubiquitous phrase *back to basics* ignites supporters. The reasonableness of returning to previously successful approaches, principles, or ethics is a tantalizing concept for solving individual or collective woes. But the "basics" that will get results for your Trust, Inc. are *far from basic*.

Leadership is not as simple as it once was. According to the Edelman Trust Barometer, "Official company-issued communications are distrusted by workers at all levels. Only 29 percent of executives and 21 percent of workers trust corporate communications."[1] Many view communications as spin-spin-spin; others, noise-noise-noise. But, the sobering challenge for leaders goes deeper. Globally, "only 18 percent of the general population trust business leaders to tell the truth regardless of how complex or unpopular the truth is."[2]

Communication that sparks trust and enables a culture of passion, engagement, and innovation requires believability. No longer does organizational spin calm rumors, nor one-way communication fuel results. No longer can bosses announce initiatives and expect quick staff alignment. And no longer are leaders able to ignore messages they don't want to address, or voices they don't want to hear—not if they want followers and credibility.

No matter what you think of discussion boards, bloggers, social media sites, text messaging, tweeting, or YouTubing, one thing is clear: Communication has changed. Technology provides instant access to alternative perspectives, influence, and thinking. The question isn't whether to get back to communication basics, but *What are the new basics?*

Although effective communication can get you above the noise, *elevated* communication is an essential ingredient to building trust. Elevated communication lifts understanding, creates aligned purpose, increases engagement, and kindles innovation. It improves relationships, enables healthy and productive conflict, and uses differences to heighten results. *Elevated communication is a new basic.*

What does it look like to elevate communication? And how do you elevate yours? That's what you'll find in this chapter. Elevated communication includes everything from the art of asking the right questions to thoughtful transparency, but it's grounded in four pillars: authenticity, compassion, integrity, and intention.

BEYOND THE NOISE

Pass-along tips and hot trends fill e-mails, articles, meetings, and training classes. They masquerade as secret ingredients essential for leadership heights, techniques to reduce problems with difficult coworkers, or solutions for juggling more work. Often over-hyped, they create more noise than results.

Getting your communication beyond that noise is the first step to elevating communication. To raise the bar for communication that brings understanding, natural followership, and trust, start with three basics:

1. Know what matters to those around you.

2. Be about dialogue.

3. Contribute gratitude.

Know What Matters to Those Around You

Complicating communication is a phenomenon professors Elizabeth Wolfe Morrison and Francis J. Milliken call "organizational silence." They argue, "there are powerful forces operating in organizations that can make employees feel that speaking up about issues and problems is futile, or, worse yet, dangerous."[3] They identify two sources: (1) management practices, specifically rejecting or responding negatively to dissent or negative feedback, and (2) managers' beliefs. When managers "believe employees are self-interested and untrustworthy, they will then act in ways that implicitly and explicitly discourage upward communication."[4] Low trust and low commitment results.

Contrast that approach with Google's (the number-one company to work for in 2013): "Every Friday without fail, company leaders, including [founders] Page and Brin, conduct employee forums and respond to the top 20 most-asked questions."[5] Tuning in to understand what matters to those you lead is an essential fueling trust. If you don't know what matters to the people you lead, what does that communicate about their value to you?

Be About Dialogue

Conversation is a process by which people come to understand each other better, by sharing ideas and points of view, and is an essential part of your Trust, Inc. basics, but *dialogue* elevates communication. It involves a mindful exchange without preconceived agendas. Dialogue is a way of hearing and contributing to a collective wisdom, without judgment, a need to "win," or believing you have *the* answer. In some ways, it's thinking together, and in doing so opening new possibilities and new voices.

Diana Chapman Walsh, former president of Wellesley College, describes it this way: "It's when we let our guard down and allow our differences and doubts to surface and interact that something authentic and original can begin to emerge, tentatively, in the spaces between us."[6] At its heart, it involves what The Center for Ethical Leadership calls a "gracious space." Being in dialogue means opening yourself to differences and a greater common good. It involves authentic interaction and trust.

Contribute Gratitude

It's common sense to show appreciation, to let people know they're valued, and to say thank you. But, some leaders believe it's unnecessary because employees are "just doing their jobs."

An American Psychological Association survey confirms the power of common sense—that employees who feel valued do better work—"Almost all employees (93 percent) who reported feeling valued said that they are motivated to do their best at work and 88 percent reported feeling engaged."[7] Yet, sincere, specific, and personal appreciation that builds trust and elevates communication is the opposite of what happens in many work groups where robotic awards, canned programs, and generic messages are the norm.

Contributing gratitude starts with focused noticing—and a thank-you. *Thank you for taking on additional tasks during the hiring freeze; thank you for giving up your weekend to finish the proposal; thank you for an exceptional job dealing with that customer problem.* Giving genuine, heartfelt, honest appreciation elevates mood, heightens self-worth, and triggers positive behaviors. Harvard associate professor Francesca Gino calls it "the gratitude effect." One of her studies involved salaried fundraisers who were either thanked or not thanked for their hard work by the director. The results? "The expression of gratitude increased the number of calls by more than 50 percent" for the week; calls made by those not thanked didn't change from the prior week.[8]

When people think communication is about communication*s*—in other words, the methods by which information is shared—rather than honest conversation and understanding, communication isn't elevated. When people require staff to hear information from "those they trust," but spin the truth in such a manner that those doing the telling are asked to compromise integrity in the process, communication isn't elevated. And when communication stems from a desire to cajole, fool, control, or manipulate, communication isn't elevated.

Elevated communication is well-intentioned, selfless, and other-focused. It enables, not inhibits others. Management guru Peter Drucker positions it this way: "Communications always makes demands. It always demands that the recipient become somebody, do something, believe something. It always appeals to motivation. If, in other words, communication fits in with the aspirations, the values, the purposes of the recipient, it is powerful. If it goes against his aspirations, his values, his motivations, it is likely not to be received at all, or, at best, to be resisted."[9]

Elevated communication brings honesty, integrity, authenticity, and caring into the conversation. It springs from a best-self connection, in the deepest sense. It lifts relationships with trust, connection, and shared experiences.

THOUGHTFUL TRANSPARENCY

As with accountability, people want *other* people, not always themselves, to be transparent. Take the example of a Kickstarter campaign by a 9-year-old wanting to raise money to go to a university camp to study computer games. She wanted to prove to her brothers that she was smart too, and could design her own game. More than $20,000 was raised to support her aspirations. But when crowdfunding supporters learned, via a Reddit staffer, that her mother was a multimillionaire entrepreneur, the dynamic shifted. As one headline put it, "The Kickstarter Principle: Crowdfunding Doesn't Work Without Transparency and Trust."[10] Neither does elevated communication.

If the mother had been forthcoming about her own status, and said the campaign wasn't about tuition affordability but rather a desire to help her daughter learn how to stand up for herself, then those contributing could have made an informed judgment about whether or not to donate.

Contrast that mother's withholding of pertinent information with a bookstore owner's approach. Faced with closing her independent bookstore for lack of cash flow, she decided to explain the situation and ask the store's 500 best customers to spend more—$35 each a month or a $100 gift card purchase. When asked about the approach, the store owner said, "I was very careful about how I phrased it, which is that we had no more to give. I didn't want people to feel like they were being coerced. I have a lot of gratitude for the community and I wanted to come from that perspective."[11] Her elevated communication and transparency started a spread-the-message campaign by customers and the bookstore was saved.

Transparency at Work

What does transparency mean for you and your Trust, Inc.? It's complicated—but you knew that, right? There are those who see transparency as open-book management, others as translucent information sharing, especially between departments. Some consider it as fair processes in decision-making and rewards and resource allocation; others as "no more secrets." The ways of being transparent at work are as different as the people who call for the transparency.

Some think transparency applies just to financial disclosure to investors, regulatory compliance, or economics, such that "a market is transparent if much is known by many." Others think transparency is the eliminating of hidden agendas, or "operating in such a way that it is easy for others to see what actions are performed."[12] Still others think it's a buzzword, such as the "transparency clash" that occurred when reporters were not given the "right" to watch President Obama play golf with Tiger Woods.

There are those who find transparency threatening; others exhilarating. Some confuse transparency with authenticity, or think transparency means communicating everything or knowing everything *they* want to know. Curious times we live in—on one hand transparency is a hot topic and there are cries for more of it; on the other, people proliferate rude, inappropriate, or mean-spirited barrages behind *anonymous* twitter handles, postings, and e-mail.

In the context of creating authentic trust in your trust-pocket, transparency isn't knowing everything or telling everything. It's creating an environment where people can trust that they'll have the pertinent information they need to do great work, make informed decisions, enter into genuine relationships, and operate with self-alignment and integrity. Thoughtful transparency increases authentic trust.

REFLECTIVE EXERCISE
Does This Transparency Increase Trust?

Mark those situations you think describe a transparency that would increase your trust as a leader.

1. During a performance discussion, you give a star staff member an average increase, telling her you're disappointed, but were unable to get the amount you wanted approved by your boss.

2. You confide in a colleague about difficulties you're having with a peer. A few weeks later, the difficult peer mentions he was surprised to hear you found him hard to work with. You discuss with the original colleague her breaking of your confidence.

3. During an employee meeting, you're asked about the possibility of staff cutbacks. You're aware it's being discussed and feel you owe it to your staff to give them a heads up, so you do, even though you were asked to keep the information confidential.

4. You don't know how to do something your boss asked you to do. You've tried to figure it out, but don't know where to start or whom to ask for help. You tell him.

5. Your team has worked hard on a big contract proposal for a client and it's now down to you and another competitor. During presentation preparations, a staff member identifies a major flaw in your plan. You ask your team to correct it, and immediately notify the potential client of the change.

6. A member of your team casually shares with you and a few coworkers examples of inappropriate business conduct by a company director on a recruiting trip to a local college. You saw something similar last year, but still feel it's none of your business.

7. You're furious about a new policy that's about to be implemented. When asked what you think at a staff meeting, you tell your staff in unmitigated terms what you do, indeed, think.

8. You're having a few beers with other managers. People start swapping idiot-boss stories. You have a few you could share about your boss, but don't.

9. Your boss's boss has a nephew interviewing for a position in your department. You don't think he's a good candidate. When your boss stops in and tells you glowing things about the young man, you agree to hire him, without ever voicing your concerns.

10. You have information that might change a company decision about a product launch. No one has asked for your opinion. You decide it's important to share what you know with appropriate decision makers.

Self-scoring: Your chances of increasing trust would be enhanced with the kind of transparency described in 2, 4, 5, 8, and 10. These are examples of thoughtful transparency.

Thoughtful transparency enhances trust because it builds confidence in your good judgment, integrity, and positive intentions. People who operate with thoughtful transparency consider the reason for forthright communication; the purpose, as it were. As long as that purpose isn't self-serving and is grounded in doing what's right without violating confidentiality, it's thoughtful transparency. If communication shifts to a self-serving agenda, or an attitude of "tell everything you know regardless of the impact on others or the purpose behind it," it's far from elevated. So how do you do this? How do you create a sense of transparency—honest communication that elevates the connection, message, and trust?

Transparency Tips That Elevate Communication

❖ **Vulnerable storytelling.** I was a senior manager for a national company before I ever shared with staff that despite a bachelors from Stanford and a masters from the University of Michigan, I'd been fired from my first professional job. At the time, I didn't even tell my parents. The shame and embarrassment haunted me for years. But eventually I realized that such failing experiences in my career had been stepping stones for success and were worth sharing. University of Houston Professor Brené Brown puts it this way in her book *Daring Greatly*: "Vulnerability is about sharing our feelings and our experiences with people who have earned the right to hear them. Being vulnerable and open is mutual and an integral part of the trust-building process." The key is "sharing appropriately," she says, adding that "Vulnerability without boundaries leads to disconnection, distrust, and disengagement."[13] It's not comfortable to be vulnerable. Yet in that discomfort, the honest and appropriate sharing of our own "truths" can create deep connections and elevate communication.

❖ **The know-but-can't-share dilemma.** Where does transparency fit into confidentiality? There's information you know and information you can tell. Sometimes they're the same; sometimes not. Confidentiality has an important place at work. You can't have authentic trust and genuine relationships without a practice that involves confidentiality. Sometimes you can reference that you're not at liberty to talk about something; other times even that's not possible. In the words of former Secretary of State Hillary Rodham Clinton, "In almost every profession—whether it's law or journalism, finance or medicine or academia or running a small business—people rely on the space of trust that confidentiality provides. When someone breaches that trust, we are all worse off for it."[14]

❖ **Feedback and a realm of truth.** Do you tell your friend, "That dress does nothing for you," or go along with what she likes? Do you let a staff member know his aspirations for promotion aren't going to happen if he stays working for you, so he can look elsewhere, or do you allow him to harbor a dream because you don't want to lose him? Do you share with a peer critique that came up about her department, or assume she already knows? Feedback can be a challenge to give and receive. If you want elevated communication, you need people who have the courage to tell you "the truth," as they see it. Find people to work with who want the best for you, and have the courage to return that favor. When you want the best for others, feedback springs from a place of integrity. It's kind, considerate, and helpful, and it builds trust. Feedback is opinion, not fact, and when offered with compassionate intention, it's also a gift. I'm indebted to people who've had the courage to tell me things that were hard for them to say and for me to hear. They changed my career (and my life) for the better.

❖ **Handling the impromptu with ease and grace.** There's a pause, a collective silence, that occurs after someone raises an issue or asks a question in a public forum that puts you, their leader, on edge. It may feel like it's a damned-if-you-do and damned-if-you-don't moment. The easy out involves "a little lie" or "stretching of truth," or saying "it's still under discussion," even when it's not. Nineteenth-century essayist Adrienne Rich said, "Lying is done with words, and also with silence." Some leaders do both. They buy time by feigning no knowledge, ignoring the question, or passing off to someone else. Those who build trust understand the stakes are high. Lie, and trust is diminished; come from a place of honesty and openness, and it flourishes. These are the times when connecting to your authentic self (see Chapter 9) as you speak shifts both your response and the way it's heard. Nothing elevates communication faster than authenticity. You know when you're being authentic—when it feels like ease and grace to both speaker and listener.

Responses to transparency aren't always what we expect. Some light up the Twitterverse, produce visits to Human Resources, or fuel rumors. But if you come from a place of thoughtful transparency, you'll find a different kind of value. In the words of Brené Brown, "What we know matters, but who we are matters more. *Being* rather than *knowing* requires showing up and letting ourselves be seen. It requires us to dare greatly, to be vulnerable"[15] [italics added].

TRUST-REDUCERS: HOW NOT TO COMMUNICATE

If we asked random work groups to name *communication behaviors leaders use that diminish trust*, they would list dozens and dozens, but many fall into similar categories. Following are trust-reducers representative of what we'd hear, intended as a nudge to all Trust, Inc. leaders to ask, "Do I do this?"

- **The all-about-me-channel.** Dominating the conversation, these leaders are addicted to their opinions, thoughts, and interests. According to them, they have the right answers, the latest gadgets, and the newest trends. They talk more than listen, and wouldn't think to ask your opinion or begin a conversation with an engaging question.

- **A one-size-fits-all approach.** They talk about employees as interchangeable game pieces, seeing people by their generation, gender, or role. Their communication is generic and impersonal. They couldn't name your significant other or what interests, aspirations, or life challenges you have. You're a means to their end; nothing personal.

- **Misplaced attention.** Ignorant of what it means to "be here now," these people are anywhere but "here." They're texting, chatting on the phone, reading an e-mail, or otherwise engaged with something other than the person in front of them. You'll see them at dinner with their children checking e-mail, holding up a line while texting, or ignoring a flight attendant's "devices off" message.

- **Letting issues fester.** Believing *If you ignore it, it'll go away*, these leaders avoid conflict, don't address issues directly, and say they don't want to hear about problems, so "work it out." They don't want to be involved, and offer little support. You can't count on them for assistance in or out of your department because when issues get challenging, they back away.

- **The forgetfulness syndrome.** It's convenient what these people "can't remember saying" or committing to. They're exceptional in convincing you that you "got it wrong" or misunderstood what they said. Their commitments and positions are ever shifting. They're expert weasel-word users—words such as *should, maybe, might,* or *try*, which suck the meaning out of perfectly good sentences.

- **Using the wrong method for the message.** These people send text messages similar to the one my friend's son received telling him he didn't need to come in Monday because he no longer had a job. They think any message can be electronically communicated in one-way approaches because a policy change, salary reduction, or responsibility reshuffle is easier without pushback. To them, face-to-face communication is a waste of their time.

- **Stirring the e-mail pot.** There's not a capital letter these people dislike, or an e-mail thrashing they haven't attempted. Their words can be thoughtless, sarcastic, or demeaning. They wait until a project nears its end before jumping in to review, comment on, or look at what has evolved. Then they send a broadcast e-mail to everyone involved about what they disagree with, what's wrong, and what needs changing. They're chaos-makers, and opening an e-mail from them rarely brings joy.

The common thread to trust-reducing communication is this: It lowers, not lifts, understanding, commitment, engagement, and relationships.

TRUST-ENHANCERS: HOW TO COMMUNICATE

The chicken or the egg? Does trust enable elevated communication or does elevated communication enable the building of trusted relationships? Both. In general, you can develop a foundation for trust-enhancing communication using approaches like these:

Build Trust Using These Communication Practices
✓ Share information that's consistently credible, factual, and useful.
✓ Include honest statements: *I don't know; I made a mistake; I was wrong; I changed my mind.*
✓ Listen with undivided and focused attention.
✓ Eliminate spin, organizational speak, and buzzwords.
✓ Offer opinions as opinions, not facts.
✓ Choose words wisely—they matter.
✓ Don't let rumors come true in your work group.
✓ Be accessible, reachable, and polite.
✓ Ask questions out of curiosity; ask questions to engage; ask questions to learn.
✓ Use mistakes for teaching and as opportunities for professional development.

✓	Encourage and support all methods of communication; tailor to others' preferences.
✓	Reframe issues to bring about solutions and ideas.
✓	Actively look for and consider different points of view.
✓	Don't take yourself too seriously; be humble and genuine.
✓	Help people see "what it looks like"; paint word pictures to make it seeable, doable, purposeful.
✓	Use differences to create understanding; operate with healthy conflict.
✓	Reflect back what you heard; be empathetic, demonstrate care and compassion.
✓	Communicate what you're for—what you want to bring about, what matters to you.

Trust-Enhancing Tips

❖ **Make it continuous.** There's no on-off switch for trust-building communications. Think regular and ongoing. If you communicate only when you need something or when it's in your interests to tell staff, you'll limit trust. Instead, be a regular conduit for needed information.

❖ **Make it timely.** Work happens in real time. Don't wait to package information until you know everything. Keep people updated on issues pertinent to their responsibilities. Tell both good and bad news. Not knowing *critical* information is a trust-buster.

❖ **Make it honest.** Model the integrity, forthrightness, and honesty you want from others by your communication style. Expect and give honest answers. Cultivate open dialogue, regular conversations, and deep listening. Talk about trust-enhancing and trust-diminishing behaviors.

❖ **Make it *why*-based.** Basic information and direction is easy—for example, telling people what you want. Now offer the why. Help others understand how what they do fits into a bigger vision. Tasks without purpose impede engagement; changes without reasons leave people guessing; deadlines without the thinking behind them don't elicit commitment. People need the *why* behind the *what*.

❖ **Make it yours.** How you handle difficult communication is itself a message. Don't delegate delivery. Messages of serious critique, shortcomings, employment termination, unpopular policy, or organizational change can be difficult. Let your actions be a message of respect, caring, and compassion.

People operating with elevated communication are realists. They understand they have bad days, tempers can flare, words can be more caustic than intended, and life issues can distract. They realize they don't always show up with their best self, know the right words to use in a difficult conversation, or handle a crisis in the best way. But they do know that although communication may not always be elevated, it can be honest, and in its imperfection, authentic.

STAYING GROUNDED

Who you are on the inside affects your behavior on the outside. You can't touch others with elevated communication unless you're operating from a grounded best-of-self place—your authentic core. There's a saying about writers: If the writer cries when writing a piece, the reader can feel her tears. It's the same concept with elevating communication: If you show up authentically, with compassion, positive intention, and integrity, it can open a door to others.

Similar to a road without the appropriate map-dots designating a scenic route, we see each other without any special designation. We see a role, but not always the person. Although we expect to feel awe seeing a Van Gogh or Rembrandt masterpiece or watching Olympians win gold, having a work experience where someone's words touch us, his thoughts inspire us, or her ideas amaze us, is a surprise. Yet, that's what elevated communication can do. It opens us by connecting us. And when it does, we *see* each other.

That connection doesn't happen every day, but whenever it does, it shifts our awareness about what *can be* at work. In the words of Deepak Chopra, "Knowledge of any kind...brings about a change in awareness from where it is possible to create new realities." For Trust, Inc. leaders, those new realities are vast.

CHAPTER 8
Demonstrate Behavioral Integrity

Our problem is not to find better values but to be faithful to those we profess.

~ John W. Gardner

Don't think your staff doesn't notice. They do. They hear you expound on the importance of the customer, then watch you cut staffing levels; they take note when you insist "we all" work Saturday to finish a project, then see you show up briefly; they understand you're a stickler for everyone meeting your deadlines, then are surprised when you don't meet yours and their performance appraisals are weeks late. If you don't take what you say seriously, why should they?

It's true, actions do speak louder than words, but words determine how actions are measured. People's perception of your word–action connection influences how they see you—credible or not credible, trustworthy or not trustworthy. The alignment between words and actions creates credibility, believability, and predictability—all essential for trust. That's the simple version of behavioral integrity.

Here's a broader one. Cornell University Professor Tony Simons, an expert on the topic, defines behavioral integrity as "the perceived pattern of alignment between another's words and deeds."[1] The operative word is perceived. As he explains, "The notion of 'behavioral integrity' describes the extent to which one person perceives that another lives his or her word, keeps promises, and lives professed values. Effective management leadership depends on how employees perceive their manager's behavior on these points because this drives credibility. Since most managers are neither saints nor demons, employees judge their managers' integrity by interpreting a mixed set of managerial actions and behaviors."[2]

Behavioral integrity is in the eye of the beholder. Not only do our experiences vary with the same person, but the same experience can also be interpreted differently. It can depend on our past interactions, expectations, or sensitivities. It may also be influenced by how we feel about the company or work environment. However, according to Professor Simons, one thing is clear: "Employees' perceptions of their managers' integrity deeply affects their loyalty, their commitment and their willingness to work hard."[3] Having behavioral integrity enables you to receive loyalty, commitment, and exceptional efforts. It paves the way for trusting relationships to emerge.

Behavioral integrity creates a psychological contract, of sorts. If your staff thinks you have behavioral integrity, they'll expect your promises are kept, your commitments are honored, what you say is important will be important, and how you profess you are, you are. If that doesn't happen or there are perceived violations, the effect can be significant. Part of the profound impact from the Great Recession was a broken social contract between employers and employees, resulting in significantly diminished trust.[4]

Some psychologists consider behavioral integrity a condition or antecedent to trust, others a necessary component. In either case, it's an ingredient Trust, Inc. leaders need. That's what this chapter is about, complete with ways to increase your behavioral integrity factor.

INTEGRITY OR BEHAVIORAL INTEGRITY?

When we use the word integrity, typically we mean our own or someone else's personal integrity, rather than intellectual, artistic, or professional integrity. For the purpose of understanding integrity related to trust at work, consider the difference between behavioral integrity and personal integrity.

Two articles from my local Montana paper offer real-world illustrations of this. The first involved an executive being considered for a board position with a mining company. When he was questioned about the academic degrees listed in his bio, he said that his certification as a mining engineer was "the equivalent" of the Bachelor of Science degree he listed, and his actual Master of Public Administration "included course work identical" to the MBA he listed.[5] Because personal integrity relates to a person's character, moral code, or ethical principles, most people concluded his biography demonstrated low integrity, and he withdrew from consideration. However, let's say his bio instead correctly included the mining certification and public administration degree. Now the document would demonstrate a bit of character in his honesty. But writing a biography with integrity doesn't spark trust. Being factual and honest is an expected biographical norm and doesn't award trust points.

The second story involved a county deputy attorney arrested on a Friday night for a domestic incident. While others waited in jail until Monday for normal hearing hours, a justice came to him for a special after-midnight hearing and he was released on his own recognizance. Because this deputy attorney works for a department claiming it's "about equal treatment for people regardless of what they do for a living,"[6] the situation illustrates no behavioral integrity; no word–action alignment. If the story was instead about him living the values his department holds, remaining in jail like everyone else until Monday, it would demonstrate behavioral integrity; an alignment of values professed and actions taken. That has the potential to increase his credibility and spark trust (assuming the outcome from his arrest didn't counter it). Behavioral integrity is normally demonstrated over time and in multiple ways.

Following is a multi-source composite intended as a quick way to differentiate behavioral integrity from personal integrity, and to assess the resulting impact on trustworthiness.[7]

What's the Difference?	
Behavioral Integrity	**Personal Integrity**
Based on others' perceptions; subjective	Primarily a relationship one has with oneself
Words and actions are perceived to be in alignment (in the present time or based on history)	Relates to person's character; imposes restrictions on self; self-integration
Person's stated principles, not moral principles, are used to judge his word–action agreement	Moral convictions; adherence in action to moral codes or ethical principles
Values talked about are values demonstrated and seen by others in action; self-alignment	Steadfast to identity-conferring commitments; standing for something within a moral context

| Believability, credibility, and predictability enable trust; psychological contract emerges based on trust | Integrity *alone* doesn't build trust; psychological contract not an emerging factor |

For example, if you're a vegan, you demonstrate personal integrity by not eating or using animal products. Your actions are self-integrated and based on your moral convictions. You may or may not share your beliefs with others; it's the way you orient your life according to your principles, placing restrictions on yourself to live that way. For most of your friends and colleagues, your vegan lifestyle won't increase their trust in you, though some may admire the way you live your values. Being a vegan is about how you choose to live; it's not about them. This isn't to say people with high personal integrity don't build trust—they do. But their personal integrity by itself isn't enough. They must also demonstrate behavioral integrity.

Behavioral integrity isn't grounded in what you believe is morally right or wrong—after all, you may believe one thing and say another. It's judged against the backdrop of your words, not unspoken values, standards, or principles. Behavioral integrity isn't doing what's right (although that's always helpful), but actually doing what you say you'll do. The question is, are you good to your word?

Let's say your 4-year-old refuses to pick up her toys, throwing a tired tantrum. You tell her that she won't get a bedtime story unless she does. Eventually, you acquiescence and take her to bed, reading her a story even though she didn't pick up her toys, because it helps her fall asleep. There's no moral issue here; there's a behavior-consistency one: What you said and what you did were not aligned. Is this a rare or regular event? Will she believe you the next time you tell her there's a consequence? The frequency of alignment of your word–action behavior will guide her decision. Consistency affects the interpretation of another's behavioral integrity, positively or negatively. No consistency = no believability. No believability = no credibility. No credibility = no trust that you'll do as you say.

Even bosses without personal integrity can have behavioral integrity when words and actions are in alignment. But, if you're wondering whether someone with negative or harmful principles or despicable moral precepts can have integrity if she lives by them, the answer is no. Most who philosophize about and examine the concepts related to integrity agree that "persons of integrity may differ about what is right, but a moral monster cannot have integrity."[8]

THERE IS NO LITTLE STUFF

Bottom line? You need to demonstrate behavioral integrity to build trust. Most of us meet our big commitments and promises at work, but if you think it's only the big stuff that matters in demonstrating behavioral integrity and building trust currency, think again. Everything matters.

REFLECTIVE EXERCISE
Does it Count?

Indicate with a (+) the situations likely to create a positive perception of behavioral integrity and build trust; indicate with a (-) those likely to decrease that perception and trust.

1. The company issued a policy with spending limits for entertaining business associates. A manager discusses it with his staff, failing to mention that the limits don't apply to him.

2. A department head uses phrases like "It's important to take care of employees" and "Kindness matters." When a long-serviced employee's position is cut from his budget with a year until retirement, he lobbies peers until he uncovers a suitable position for her.

3. A project team is waiting for Zoe to finish reviewing specs needed to move the project forward, but problems erupted all day and she's behind on having the specs finished by morning, the time she promised. Zoe stays late to meet her self-imposed deadline.

4. The boss chides anyone arriving late to her meetings. She's a stickler for people being on time. Her staff notices she's frequently late to work.

5. A trip to an amusement park is hard to afford, but Jim decides to take his family. His youngest daughter recently turned 3, the age at which children no longer enter for free. Although he nudges his kids to be honest, he tells the cashier his daughter won't be 3 until next week.

6. At a department meeting Joslyn offers to compile notes and commitments and send them out. Two days later, no information has arrived.

7. Customer focus is a company value regularly discussed at meetings and in communications. Two supervisors on their way to lunch see a line of customers and stop to help.

Self-scoring: Give yourself one point for a (+) for 2, 3, and 7, and one point for a (-) for 1, 4, 5, and 6. A score of 6 or better is a good indicator you're aware there's no little stuff when it comes to trust-building.

A statement indicative of our times, which should resonate regardless of your political affiliation, came from a GOP pollster who remarked, "We're not going to let our campaign be dictated by fact-checkers."[9] That's the opposite of what people need at work; they need "the facts" of what someone said compared to what he did. In this complex world in which it's hard to differentiate truth from manipulation, word–action alignment is one way to access trustworthiness. Behavioral integrity is rooted in actual actions. In the case of Trust, Inc., it's *your* actions.

Ways to Increase Your Behavioral Integrity Factor

❖ **Eliminate shape-shifting.** When you behave as expected, it increases behavioral integrity. Like a WYSIWYG person— What You See Is What You Get—consistent people don't shift positions, values, or behaviors with the latest fads, initiatives, or pressures. Their behavior is dependable. I once worked for someone who rarely gave answers on people issues in an initial discussion. Instead, she said she'd "think it through." That predictable approach demonstrated her often-referenced philosophy that people matter. Her behavior confirmed she took extra care when decisions might impact them.

❖ **Declare your intention.** Especially in times of change or new initiatives, a way to demonstrate behavioral integrity is to state your intention. Why are you doing this? What do you hope to accomplish? Is your intention to cut unnecessary expenses in support of a directive, or find funds to launch a team idea? Is your intention to hire the best candidate no matter the source, or provide a developmental opportunity for an internal person? Whatever it is, once you declare it, people stop guessing and look for word–action alignment. Trust is built when actions match stated intentions.

❖ **Choose *should* over *can*.** In the television show *The Tudors*, one of Henry VIII's newly minted wives remarked to a recently disenfranchised acquaintance, "I *can* because I can." Her words represent the philosophy of many recently crowned or well-seasoned bosses: They view themselves as having different rules, privileges, and standards. And depending on position, that's true. There are things you *can* do, but are they things you *should* do? Should you give up 5 percent of your salary when non-managers have a forced pay cut? Should you stay late when you're asking staff to? You decide. But when the issue is behavioral integrity and trust, consider carefully. If you tell your team you're a team, and don't show up as part of it Saturday, your problem may be larger than missing part of a weekend. Actions speak.

❖ **Watch for spillover.** The stories you tell, the links you send, the jokes you laugh at, the pictures you post, the causes you support, and the articles you talk about all communicate about you. Consider these as equivalent to your words. They're a way for people to judge who you say you are and who you really are; what you say you value and what you actually value. A casual business associate of mine forwarded an e-mail to his distribution list, which included me, letting us know about a resource for getting hundreds to thousands of "'likes' in just a few days" for a public Facebook page, viewers for a YouTube channel, or followers on Twitter. Really? This came from a guy who claims he's about "brand integrity."

❖ **Capture your words.** Your words have greater impact because you're someone's boss. Even if you casually mentioned she'll have an answer next week, she hears a commitment. If it's something important, it might be taken as a promise. Listen to your words. If you say you'll get back to someone tomorrow, log it on tomorrow's calendar. If you tell a peer your team will deliver information by Monday, but you mean "around Monday," he heard what you said, not what you meant. With apps to prod, organize, and schedule you, it's easy to track anything you commit to. As author Brian Tracy said, "In the area of personal credibility, the rule is everything counts." All your words do.

❖ **Get ducks in a row.** What are the three priorities for your team? How do they align with where you spend time, and what you talk about and reward? Do you evaluate staff on contributions to the department's objectives? Do they get feedback on how they operate within company values? Are performance appraisals connected to what matters? Are promotions? Behavioral integrity means having ducks aligned. Policies, procedures, rewards, and recognition approaches should match what you say matters.

❖ **Stomp out hype.** Overpromising and under-delivering destroys behavioral integrity and trust. That can include visioning. When you talk about the future, increase your clarity. People can misinterpret what *can* or *might* be for what *will* be. You create influence, build natural followership, and spark trust when your behaviors communicate the values you hold, the person you are, and the things that matter. That requires concerted and constant efforts to eliminate hype. A promise is a big deal. Don't make ones you can't keep. In the words of famed advertising guru David Ogilvy, "In the best institutions, promises are kept, no matter what the cost in agony and overtime." They're kept in the best work groups too.

❖ **Seek observers.** Whether you use a mentor or coach, or exchange favors with a colleague or professional friend, ask someone to occasionally observe you to provide alignment feedback. Where are your words and actions aligned? Where aren't they? Do you follow through on what's said? What's your behavioral integrity rating? Now go further. Evaluate your trust-pocket's behavioral integrity. Do internal or external customers think your work group honors commitments? Lives its values? Under-promises and over-delivers?

How is your Trust, Inc. word–action alignment perceived by stakeholders? Include the topic in meetings. To make behavioral integrity a trust essential, treat it as the priority it is.

Should you have fleeting thoughts that behavioral integrity isn't a bottom-line issue or doesn't matter much—that it's among the softer, intangible stuff—then consider its more tangible benefit. A study by Professor Simons found, "an improvement of only one-eighth of a point in the behavioral integrity score of a hotel's managers led to a boost in hotel profits of as much as 2.5 percent of revenues."[10]

YOUR SILENCE SPEAKS TOO

If you tell staff you'll talk to your boss about something affecting them, but never do, your silence speaks. If someone raises an important issue you ignore, your silence speaks. And if you allow practices to continue against organizational values or ethical standards without registering concern, your silence speaks. Martin Luther King, Jr., said, "In the end, we will remember not the words of our enemies, but the silence of our friends."

What you don't do is as memorable to others as what you do. When your word–action alignment is silent when it matters, the unintended consequence is this: There is no Trust, Inc. There is no trust without behavioral integrity. The good news is perceptions about behavioral integrity aren't usually established through one incident; they evolve over time from a composite of experiences. But the trust standard others set is high.

REFLECTIVE THINKING
Through Their Eyes

Consider these questions through the eyes of your staff. Writing answers can increase insight.

1. At a meeting with your staff present, your boss does a 180 on a project your

department has invested hundreds of hours working on. It's clear the decision eliminates bonus eligibility. Several peers speak up; you don't, deciding to address it with your boss later. Based on past experiences, what will your staff be saying or thinking about your behavior?

2. You authorize staff comp-time to make up for six-day weeks. Human Resources issued a memo saying compensatory time is in violation of company policy. You're asked about it at a staff meeting and say you'll address it with HR, but don't. What will your staff think when there's no answer forthcoming?

3. There's pressure to support a new initiative that's against your personal values and beliefs, which are widely known by your team. You feel you're risking a big promotion if you don't support it, so you quietly decide to go along. When your staff is asked why their boss didn't stand up against this, what do you think they'll say?

Unanticipated or unexpected consequences of silence aren't top of mind when we're juggling work and home priorities, running a business, leading a group, or trying to successfully maneuver in a work world filled with twists, turns, and potholes. But sometimes it gives us pause. That happened to me. Seated at a window table of a nice hotel restaurant, tired after an emotionally grueling day dealing with eldercare and family dynamics, my husband and I were enjoying a glass of wine and unwinding. Rambunctious children seated at a nearby table drew our attention as their antics increased. Only when the spirited brothers headed across the room and began climbing the fireplace did we hear their father calling across the restaurant. Again and again he bellowed at his children, disrupting whatever enjoyment diners had until then. Once they returned to their table, a silverware sword fight began, unheeded by either parent, followed by seat-jumping.

My irritated husband was clamoring to say something to the parents. Not wanting to draw attention to us, make a scene, or inspire restaurant rage, I convinced him not to. We hurriedly finished dinner and returned to our room. It wasn't the evening we'd planned, but it was an evening of second thoughts and reflections about my own behavioral integrity. Does disruption to 30 people by two unruly children matter enough to say something? How about a movie experience ruined by loud, incessantly talking people? Do you ask them to quiet down? What about passengers who ignore flight attendants' instructions to stay seated after landing so EMTs can board to assist a seriously ill passenger? When do you speak up?

At work, if we go along with policies that break commitments or reward behaviors counter to our professed values, what happens to our behavioral integrity? What happens if pressures dictate responses, or we stop challenging decisions negatively impacting our team or running counter to good management practices? What happens if unintended consequences of our silence bankrupts trust currency, bringing cries of hypocrisy? What happens when self-preservation trumps self-convictions? What happens when we become part of the problem?

It's simple. In the realm of trust-building, quiet compliance quickly alters perceptions about behavioral integrity. At those times people look to see if they can glimpse who we truly are.

In that contemplative evening, it hit me—if we won't speak up politely on the small issues, or if we muzzle those who would, out of fear, embarrassment, or personal concern, what will we do on bigger issues and injustices plaguing our world? Will we silently watch? Pretend them away? Ignore them? And if we do, what does that communicate about who we are? When is it important enough to stand up for something beyond self? For the greater good?

If we look the other way too often, without even registering our concerns, we compromise who we are and who we're capable of becoming. We impact those who believe in us, trust us, and look to us to lead with integrity—both with the personal integrity of doing what's right and the behavioral integrity of demonstrating through actions what we profess. The unintended consequence of that isn't just losing the trust of those we lead; it's losing our own grounding and self-trust.

IF WALLS COULD TALK

Another story from my local paper sums up a challenge we share. It involved a state school superintendent who "wrote" a column about school safety for the school's monthly newsletter. Pressed for time, he cut and pasted every word of a piece written by a Georgia educator, omitting from the story only the numbers of police officers and schools in the Georgia district. He added his name and school district and sent it to the paper as his. Once discovered, he apologized, saying "he knew what he did was wrong, but he was in a rush."[11]

Here's the challenge: That story (and thousands like it) impacts all of us as leaders. Our individual and collective stories (our actions) create a patchwork of perceptions others use to determine if they should give their trust to us as individuals or as a group. Currently, our collective report card has a failing grade on demonstrating behavioral integrity:

- "54 percent of Americans have personally observed or have firsthand knowledge of wrongdoing in the workplace."[12]

- "12 percent of employees believe their employer genuinely listens to and cares" about them.[13]

- "7 percent completely trust their employers to look out for their best interests."[14]

- "64 percent believe illegal or unethical corporate conduct was a significant factor in bringing about the economic crisis."[15]

- "Slightly more than one in 10 Americans (14 percent) believes their company's leaders are ethical and honest."[16]

The question is, if your walls could talk, if they could play back the reality of what you say and what you do on a daily basis, what stories would they tell about you? Would these stories build or diminish your trust?

In the words of George Halas, a 20th-century coach and pioneer in professional football, "Nobody who ever gave his best regretted it." Those who lead thriving trust-pockets, igniting passion, engagement, and innovation, know the stories their walls tell are stories countering that collective report card and building trust in alignment with words and actions. They know it's hard to go wrong when you give your best to both your words *and* your actions.

CHAPTER 9
Show Up Authentically

Twenty years from now you will be more disappointed by the things you didn't do than by the ones you did.

~ H. Jackson Brown

I don't know what possessed me. I'd never attempted anything like it, and I'm not a craft person. But I decided I *had* to—I just had to build a doll house. Not any doll house, mind you, but a two-story Victorian, in an expensive kit with intricate detailing and wiring. I envisioned its finished magnificence, savoring thoughts of tiny-furniture shopping and miniature-house decorating.

After reading the directions, sorting the wooden pieces, and coating them with primer, I discovered it was more complicated and time consuming than I'd considered. Following weeks of after-work play, there was limited progress. Six months later, I packed up the pieces, rationalizing that it wasn't the right time for doll-house build-ing. The right time never came, and five years later I sold the kit at a garage sale, having learned more about who I was and wasn't.

It's not unusual for me to fall in love with the *idea* of what in-trigues or challenges me. An illusion grabs me—floating dreams of the romantic side of hiking the Appalachian Trail, living a fairy-tale life in an *Architectural Digest*–type home, or writing a literary masterpiece. Typically I catch myself, and can differentiate my life from someone else's. But, sometimes I don't—such as with that doll house. Sometimes, the I-would-like-to-be-like-that delusion hijacks the sanity of knowing who I am, influencing choices and teasing me to consider different or grander paths.

However, they're usually not better or grander *for me*. Through-out the years, I've discovered my authentic me doesn't want a fancy house. I'm more of a "cottage filled with books, pictures, and things I love" type person. I know I won't write a literary masterpiece because that's not my writing style or passion. And the Appalachian Trail? Nope. I like hiking more than camping, so exploring from a wilder-ness lodge with indoor plumbing is more me.

What does any of this have to do with sparking trust-building as a Trust, Inc. leader? Everything. In a world where it's difficult to differentiate true from faux in both messages and messengers, people who show up authentically stand out. Their genuine, self-aware, honest, and consistent understanding of who they are, and how they demonstrate that authenticity in their sphere of influence, is trust-building.

In a work world as complicated as the one you work in, where competing interests, changing priorities, personal agendas, matrix reporting, and rampant misinformation churns amidst pressure to do more, those who show up authentically have an advantage. These people operate with genuine relationships, trust currency, and en-gaged staffs. They use an inner guide for grounding, while others flounder in uncertainty. They understand it's the messenger, not the message, whose authenticity sparks trust and inspires others to great work. The bottom line is this: Authentic people create authentic trust.

But, what does it look like to operate with authenticity at work? How does showing up authentically spark authentic trust? One of the joys to life and work is claiming who you are. But you can't do that, and figure out what that means for you and your work, unless you're *mindfully self-aware*. This chapter explores these topics and more.

ARE YOU SHOWING UP?

I've grown accustomed to eyes-down, face-in-gadget encounters with people too absorbed in texting to answer their child's persistent query at a store, too engrossed with e-mail to notice they're blocking the aisle, or too immersed in talking on a cell phone to respond to a food server. From personal YouTube channels to picture-posting Facebookers obsessed with documenting their day, we're enthralled with ourselves.

But you can't be authentic if you're self-absorbed. Self-awareness and self-absorption lead to different outcomes. The first builds trust; the second diminishes it. Prolific me-focused behaviors run counter to an essential for sparking trust: showing up authentically.

What does it mean to "show up authentically"? Here's my definition from *The Titleless Leader*: "Showing up means operating from your authentic self—the best of who you are at a core level. The best you includes characteristics such as: kindness, compassion, love, tolerance, trust, and integrity. It includes your uniqueness: gifts, abilities, knowledge, and inner awareness."[1] The composite of all things *you* comprises your essential nature. Authenticity involves that nature and is typically defined as "the degree to which one is true to one's own personality, spirit, or character, despite external pressures."[2]

However, *showing up authentically* in your work is different from just "being true to yourself," or responding without self-awareness or filters in accordance with how you feel, what you believe, or what you want, which can translate into myopic self-centeredness or ego-attached behaviors. It's more than knowing yourself or being you.

It involves connecting to the best of who you are at a core level. And when you're connected to that core, you can tap your inner greatness.

Showing up authentically isn't you on a desert island; it's you as authentic in yourself in a bigger world of people, who also have desires, values, needs, interests, perspectives, and authentic selves. That requires an awareness of and involvement with others and an absence of self-deception, both about who you are and how your actions impact. It requires new skills for new times.

Operating As an Authentic Boss

Psychologist Bruce Avolio and his research colleagues consider authentic leadership to be a "root construct capable of grounding other leadership frameworks." Research has determined authentic leaders can be "directive, participative, or even authoritarian, and that these common leader behavioral styles in and of themselves do not differentiate whether a leader is authentic or inauthentic."[3] That means no matter whether your leadership style is transformational, servant, participative, or directive, you can be an authentic leader. And you'll need to be, if you want your own Trust, Inc.

What does it look like to operate as an authentic leader? These optimistic, resilient, confident, self-aware leaders with high moral principles are easy to spot. Their positive philosophies, ethics, and modeling bring high standards, principled actions, and consistent expectations to those they lead. Four characteristics are typical: "Authentic leaders are true to themselves rather than conforming to the expectations of others. They are intrinsically motivated rather than extrinsically motivated. They lead from their own point of view (moral perspective) rather than by copying others. Finally their authentic principled actions are based on their personal convictions, values, and beliefs."[4] They build trust by being *who* they authentically are.

Increasing Your Authenticity at Work

❖ **Be self-like, not saint-like.** Yes, there have been times I've cried, yelled, cursed, lost patience, shown frustration, and demonstrated behaviors I'm less than proud of at work. Apologies followed some; no one wants less-than-optimal behaviors to be defining boss moments. But we're human. Work and life dynamics aren't always well navigated, and hiding behind an "everything is okay" act is not believable. Acknowledging you had a difficult morning, or are preoccupied with family news, depending on the situation, is being self-like. No one wants a plastic boss pretending saint-like qualities. Plus, you can't fake it; people know. When you're more self-like, you're more authentic. In fact, researchers have found that "genuine emotions on the part of a leader are indicative of followers' perceptions of a leader's authenticity."[5]

❖ **There's no on–off button.** As with most things, we're not always one way or another; it's not authentic or inauthentic. There are situational gradations. Researchers describe authenticity "as existing on a continuum ranging from highly inauthentic to highly authentic. This implies individuals are not either completely authentic or completely inauthentic."[6] For example: You're likely to feel less authentic testifying in court for your company or meeting your child's principal about a disruptive incident than participating in a team meeting or attending a friend's wedding. There's no standard called "authentic" to achieve at work. Rather, focus on being self-aware to understand what situations and people affect your continuum to show up authentically.

❖ **Embrace the concept of "enough-ness."** "Fear of being ordinary" is a phrase from author and professor Brené Brown. In an interview, she talked about the concept this way: "The overwhelming message in our culture today is that an ordinary life is a meaningless life unless you are grabbing a lot of attention and you have lots of Twitter followers and Facebook fans who know everything you know."[7] That model of success runs counter to authenticity. If you copy others, trying to achieve their definition of success, through their interests and desires, you're not showing up authentically. We fear that who we are isn't enough. Yet, it's through both vulnerability and risk that authentic trust is born. In the words of Brown, "Believing that you're enough is what gives you the courage to be authentic, vulnerable, and imperfect."[8] People who show up authentically don't define who they are in terms of money, recognition, fame, or outward measures but by leaving the world a bit better for having been here.

While you change careers, body size, friends, addresses, morph interests, skills, or perspectives, and evolve thinking, understanding, and wisdom, you're still you on the inside. Whether you're working on the external you-version 2.0 or 5.0, or reinventing goals, aspirations, or connections, it's still you. The challenge is to show up more that way; a more authentic boss requires a more revealed you. As the second Secretary-General of the United Nations, Dag Hammarskjöld encouraged, "What you must dare is to be yourself."

REFLECTIVE THINKING
Authentically You?

Writing your answers can increase self-discovery and insights.

1. If you asked people who report to you to describe you—your attributes, values, and character—what would they say?

2. If you asked the person in your life with whom you're most open and vulnerable, with whom you're most "you," to describe you, what would that person say?

3. What's similar in these glimpses of you? What's different? Why is that?

4. Describe your attributes, values, and character from your own perspective. Be careful to separate how you might *like* others to see you from how you *know* yourself to authentically be.

5. What can you learn about how you're showing up at work from this? On an authenticity continuum, how do you see yourself at work?

Author Anne Morrow Lindberg wrote, "The most exhausting thing you can do is to be unauthentic." The challenge for Trust, Inc. leaders isn't just to understand authenticity and its impact on trust-building, it's learning how to operate that way as a boss. Doing that requires the skill of mindful self-awareness because being a boss isn't who you are, it's something you do.

CULTIVATING SELF-AWARENESS

Brown. Green. Blue. Yellow. Red. Black. White. With an unusual ability to change skin color, the chameleon is a lizard-family celebrity. This ability provides the lizard camouflage. However, contrary to popular belief, it's not done as a camouflaging response to surroundings. Rather, skin change reflects the chameleon's reaction to temperature, light, and mood. Its color change communicates responses to stress, excitement, temperature, lighting, other chameleons, and environmental influences.

Like the chameleon, we react to our environment, changing how we show up or act. Pressures to fit in, be recognized, or get promoted can cause us to render decisions out of character or adapt unself-like behaviors—our equivalent of changing color. These chameleon-esque transformations diminish, and at times even break, trust.

When we come to realize that who we're pretending to be or morphing into isn't who we are, that self-awareness challenges us at a core level. Author Neale Donald Walsch put it this way: "Every decision you make—every decision—is not a decision about what to do. It's a decision about who you are. When you see this, when you understand it, everything changes." That's what self-awareness brings.

There are many ways to create self-awareness, to build the skill of being mindfully aware of how you're showing up. My personal favorites are watching yourself and tapping intention.

Watching Yourself

Aristotle said "we are what we repeatedly do." We acquire habits by constantly acting in a particular way. But are your habits just habits, or are they an authentic reflection of you?

Is it your habit to say no to new ideas or out-of-the-ordinary requests because it's easier than running it past your boss or owning the accountability that comes with approving it? Is it your habit to micromanage, carefully parcel information, or withhold praise? Do you close your door to avoid interruptions? Your habits can impact how you're perceived: authentic or not, approachable or not, trustworthy or not.

It's not enough to simply think about the habits that get in our way or impact others' perceptions about us. We need to see, feel, own, and affect our habits—experience them, as if we're seeing them through someone else's eyes. Watching yourself involves a technique of stepping outside yourself to do just that—to observe yourself and your behavior, but with a twist. Most of us naturally observe ourselves at times. We use that information to improve our results. If I watch a video of me speaking, I judge what I like, don't like, and need to improve. Noticing and correcting habits and behaviors is something Trust, Inc. leaders regularly do.

Now add a conscious focus on observing actions that diminish or build trust, and you'll discover habits you never considered impacting your ability to grow your trust currency. Start by noticing the actions others do that build or diminish trust and review your behaviors in light of these. Or use behaviors from Chapter 3 and focus on one or two at a time.

Once you're doing regular self-observations, dive a little deeper. Here's the twist: enhancing authenticity through the skill of self-awareness happens without judgment. When we only see flaws, we reinforce "not enough," but when we see the wholeness of who we truly are, we experience "enough-ness."

Shift to watching yourself as though you're someone else. As if from deeper eyes, a watching, witnessing, observing self can see without judging, notice without correcting, and observe without changing. Watching yourself from this vantage point cultivates a self-awareness that reduces self-deception. When you notice yourself changing colors like a chameleon, bending to pressure against your values, or operating contrary to your character, this shift in perception enables you to glimpse how others perceive you, and you can use that information to course-correct by re-grounding yourself to the best of who you are. Showing up authentically at work isn't an absolute standard. The goal is *more often.*

10 Questions to Hone Your Self-Observation Skills
1. What impact am I having on those around me during this meeting? How am I affecting others' participation, reaction, or engagement?
2. What can I interpret from my own body language right now that others might be reading? Or misreading?
3. If I walked into a new company and watched the group leader doing what I'm doing, what would that communicate to me about her?

4.	What decisions did I make today that I'd make differently, if I could? Why is that?
5.	What have I done today that would demonstrate I value the work a staff member does?
6.	What actions have I taken recently that I'm not proud of? Why is that?
7.	What decisions or habits have I recently been demonstrating that align with my personal values and beliefs? Which don't?
8.	I look myself in the eye and ask, Where did I show up as my best self today? Where didn't I?
9.	Any chameleon-esque actions today? What might these have communicated about me that's not grounded in who I am?
10.	Ben Franklin's evening question: "What good have I done today?"

Tapping Intention

Did the man in the window seat suggest an elaborate seat change with a grandfather traveling with three grandchildren because he really wanted to assist them, or was his intention to end up in the aisle where his robust body would have more room? Only he knows. Was it your colleague's intention to withhold information you needed to do a great job on the project, or did the chaos of changing priorities cause her to forget? Only she knows. Although we speculate about others, trying to determine their motives, it's our own we should explore. The heart of your intention is found in your answer to the question, *Why am I doing this, anyway?*

Our intentions may not always be what they seem. Sometimes we fool ourselves. But when we're honest, we know if what appears to everyone else to be a kind act from us has a personal agenda attached. We know whether the policy change we're advocating is what we profess it to be, or a subtle coup. We know if volunteering for a committee is self-serving or altruistic. We know if our praise is genuine or manipulative. We know what's in our heart. We know our own intentions—at least, we do when we stop deceiving ourselves.

Early in my career my intention was to win, although I wouldn't have thought that at the time. I wanted more—more responsibilities, more rewards. But in the process of transitioning from a minimum-wage employee to a vice president of a multibillion-dollar company, I realized by having a "win" intention I was becoming someone I didn't recognize much. So, I worked first on changing my intention to a "winning" one; trying to contribute more, make a difference, and live my life's potential. The way that happened is described in my book *Hitting Your Stride: Your Work, Your Way*, but suffice it to say, learning to tap my intention enabled me to show up more authentically. That self-awareness was instrumental in changing how I chose to operate. It was after that when both my career and my life took off.

What's your goal or purpose? That's intention. What do you have in mind to bring about? That's intention. What's your motive? That's intention. Tapping intention provides a powerful mirror, and a way to move toward greater authenticity through mindful self-awareness. In the words of Henry David Thoreau, "I know of no more encouraging fact than the unquestionable ability of a man to elevate his life by conscious endeavor."

IT'S NOT ENOUGH TO WALK THE TALK

There's a difference between *acting* and *being*. Walking the talk at work can be acting, unless you work in a culture aligned with who you are or one that's at least not counter to it. If the "talk" isn't what you can authentically support, based on your values, beliefs, and principles, then your ability to build trust by showing up authentically is reduced. Yet, organizations can put leaders in that position.

Too many people are asked to manage using last-century thinking about employee motivation, or support Theory X policies designed to control and prod, when building trust-currency and creating an environment where people can be self-motivated is their way. Too many are expected to support and endorse initiatives that run counter to their thinking, or make results happen by twisting arms or mandating extra hours with tactics and approaches that grate on their compassion and sensibility. They're asked to "sell" a change even when they know everyone won't be part of its future. And most of the time, they do. They talk the talk and walk the talk.

But when that happens to us not occasionally, but again and again and again, a part of us withers, our stomach tightens, or our sleep becomes fitful. We feel inauthentic because we are. And when we compromise who we are for what we do, our staff knows it too. Acting doesn't build credibility, create followership, enhance engagement, ignite passions, or build trust. It doesn't bring sustainable results. And it certainly doesn't create a work culture in which ideas are freely shared to innovate solutions for tomorrow's needs.

In the new workplace where trust is the currency that gets results, the challenge is to walk *your* talk while still supporting the company. To *be* not only who you say you are, but who you really are. Sure, great. Sounds like motherhood and apple pie, but this is the real world of work. How do you do that?

Turning "Walk the Talk" into "Walk *Your* Talk"

❖ **Figure out where you stand.** You may know what you don't like, what you don't want, or what is against your principles. But what will you stand for? What will you work to bring about? What will cause you to speak up or lobby your boss or company leaders to change? What are you willing to develop and grow for your Trust, Inc.? Define it. Articulate it. Talk about it. Align with it. You can't walk-*your*-talk without understanding where the boundary is *for you*. Once, I changed bosses when my old one crossed a line I couldn't follow; another time I changed companies; still another I worked to evolve a culture. What are your boundaries? What will you stand *for*?

❖ **Be known as an authentic person.** Values matter. Ethics matter. Principles matter. Authenticity matters. Trust matters. But bringing it out or trying it out occasionally doesn't work. Build a reputation around who you are. That builds trust and influence. It's hard to resist input from a well-intentioned leader who's also an authentic one. These are the people whom others naturally look to and follow; people who can, by the nature of who they are, get things done. Be known for consistency, predictability, high performance, and moral character. Be known for how you show up. Be known for walking-*your*-talk.

❖ **Work in parallel.** Foolhardy actions benefit no one. Sometimes as leaders, we need to align with the directive, walk *the* talk, and move directionally in ways we wouldn't personally choose. These are times when a moral line isn't crossed for us, but a compassionate one might be. Working in parallel means helping to change what's wrong, while still supporting and operating under current standards. If your company operates with myths about what motivates employees today and you care about that, volunteer to work on a committee to help change it. If you're frustrated about asking staff to work even harder with no end in sight, develop ideas to help mitigate the pain or reward the efforts. Action feels better than inaction. Not only will your staff notice, but you will too. Incremental progress, through time, is a powerful motivator. Working in parallel allows you to walk *the* talk *and* walk *your* talk. It's a way to make a difference and show up authentically in a culture that may, on first glance, seem unresponsive to that risk. It's a way to be who you are despite broader organizational obstacles.

There are few things more powerful for trust-building than authenticity. Getting beyond walking the talk to walking *your* talk—moving from acting to being—is a way to demonstrate who you are at work. It's also a way to engage your passions. In the words of author, educator, and civil rights leader Howard Thurman, "Don't ask what the world needs. Ask what makes you come alive, and go do it. Because what the world needs is people who have come alive."

IT TAKES A LITTLE MASHING

Using tiny fingers to press a large green grape against the side of a bowl, my oldest granddaughter managed to squeeze out a bit of juice. Taking up a spoon for leveraged pressing, she extracted a bit more. Working the spoon and her fingers together she encountered even more success, adding a second grape to her labor-intensive juice-extraction experiment.

Now enthralled with the transformation of grapes to juice, she announced to the family her mission: make everyone a glass of grape juice. After negotiating permission for more grapes and a potato masher from her mother, she developed her mash-the-juice-out process, ultimately bringing juice in doll-ware glasses for the six of us. With focus and procedural enhancements along the way, she achieved her goal an hour later.

Similar to my granddaughter, we all have things that draw our attention and missions we're persuing. Some are launched from curiosity, passion, or interest; some are short-lived, some lifelong quests. Some result from the necessity of a changing world, life events, or concepts nudging us to reinvent ourselves as better, healthier, kinder, simpler, smarter, or more enhanced versions of ourselves. But often, we're just struggling to *let us out*.

No one can bring to your work exactly what you can bring in exactly the same way—your gifts, abilities, knowledge, inner awareness, and best-you characteristics are different from mine or his or hers. The question for Trust, Inc. leaders isn't how to reinvent yourself, morph yourself, or evolve yourself as a better boss. The question is, How can you *be* yourself? How can you bring the core and essence of who you are to your world?

In my way of thinking we're like my granddaughter's grapes: It takes a little mashing to discover our "juice" and bring its sweetness to the world. So despite the setbacks, challenges, problems, and hurdles work brings, consider it like grape-mashing. Every time you move your authenticity continuum up, you're bringing more of yourself—your juice—to the world. Every time you stand for what you believe, or work to bring positive change, you share more of your juice with the world. And every time you show up authentically, you build trust and make a difference by giving other people permission to do the same.

CHAPTER 10
Build Genuine Relationships

A relationship involves a lot of work and commitment.
~ Greta Scacchi

There are faux followers on Twitter, counterfeit professionals on LinkedIn, and more than 83 million fake accounts on Facebook.[1] At work the people are real enough, but not so much the relationships. In fact, a common relationship style reinforced in many work cultures is one authors Solomon & Flores call "cordial hypocrisy," in which people "pretend there is trust when there is none."[2]

There are "What can you do for me today?" relationships, competitive-adversarial ones, and "What's in it for me?" varieties. There are manipulative, bullying, and difficult relationships, countered by giving, helpful, and supportive ones. Some last a few hours; others decades. On the work relationship list are also genuine ones involving personal investments of time, commitment, energy, and trust. A genuine work relationship isn't necessarily a friendship, long-lasting, or function-specific, although it could be any of these. What determines whether it's genuine or not is its intent or purpose, and whether it's *mutually beneficial*.

Although studies confirm that "in work organizations, individuals seek to form and maintain mutually beneficial relationships with peers, superiors, and subordinates to gain instrumental assistance and social support,"[3] genuine relationships offer something more. When times are difficult, challenges overwhelming, and pressures soaring, genuine relationships can pull you and your Trust, Inc. through. These are the relationships that lift you up, help you thrive, enable your talents, and give deeper meaning to what you do.

When you can make a difference in someone's life, help him share his talents and passions, and discover he does the same or more for you, it changes your work. The how-tos behind these uncommon work relationships and why they're essential to your Trust, Inc. are the focus of this chapter. Keep in mind the chapter addresses only genuine *work* relationships. Personal relationships with significant others, family, and friends are on a different emotional bandwidth, and there's no implied overlap for approaches or messages intended here.

WHAT IS A GENUINE WORK RELATIONSHIP?

There's a difference between being "in" a relationship with someone at work, and "having" a working relationship with him or her. Here's an example: When going in and out of the building you acknowledge and speak to Lauren, a receptionist, and Josh, a security guard. Occasionally, you chat or exchange tidbits. As with others with whom you come in casual contact, you're friendly and cordial, enjoying the interaction.

However, you're not *in* a work relationship with Lauren or Josh; you're just *having* one. If either left tomorrow, you'd develop a similar relationship with whomever replaced him or her. It's not that you don't care about them, but there's no genuine relationship to have—no authentic trust is needed between you, there's no outcome to resolve, and no best you or best them to show up or engage. It's a work relationship similar to many work relationships—simple, but fleeting. It's cordial but not mutually beneficial or trust-essential.

There's nothing wrong with these work relationships; we have lots of them. But they're not the kind of relationships you need with *key* staff, peers, or bosses. Those relationships require something more—an exchange of services or skills, direction or information, collaboration, cooperation, unique contributions toward mutual goals, or investments of time, commitment, or effort.

These significant relationships affect your well-being, livelihood, development, results, and career. They matter to you in tangible *and* intangible ways. And if you want them to positively enhance your work and the thriving of your Trust, Inc., most of your key relationships should be genuine ones. However, not all desired relationships that would benefit from being genuine can be. There are two sides to a relationship: You control one, and influence the potential for reciprocity through your actions.

A Genuine Work Relationship Exists...

- **When the relationship matters more than any single outcome.** Real relationships aren't predicated on the success of a particular project, initiative, or once-and-done occurrence. Although they ebb and flow, they can weather organizational change, demanding deadlines, healthy conflict, and misunderstandings because the relationship itself matters.

- **When you want the best for the other person.** Genuine relationships aren't one-sided, but mutually beneficial. That necessitates well-meaning intentions and consciously operating with a winning philosophy akin to one I created for my life: "It's only when we're all winning that we truly all win."[4] Wanting the best for someone else shifts the orientation away from self to balanced concern for both self and others.

- **When you bring the best of who you are *into* that relationship.** When behaviors are grounded from an authentic self—the best of who you are at a core level—it raises the relationship bar, not just for you, but for others as well. That raised bar creates a greater self-awareness of how your actions impact others. It also spurs you to go first in giving, building, and repairing trust.

- **When the relationship operates with authentic trust.** The ongoing cultivation of authentic trust, and its resulting trust currency, is central to genuine work relationships. Behaviors that build and nurture authentic trust are an ongoing essential for these relationships. Genuine work relationships don't happen without trust—but, not all trusting relationships are genuine.

In a time when text messages top face-to-face or live voice-to-voice conversations, being in a relationship with others, wanting the best for them, and helping them achieve their best generates trust. It also differentiates leaders.

Reinforced by command-and-control styles, winner-take-all cultures, and us-vs.-them mindsets, the perception can be that leaders are out for themselves, using staff as a means to their ends. But those working for bosses who build genuine relationships find something quite different. As my friend and colleague Beth Pelkofsky pointed out, "Operating with genuine relationships gives bosses a big edge. It can make the difference between a good boss and a great one."[5]

Beth's right. You can't be a great boss without genuine relationships, nor can you create a trust-pocket where passion, engagement, and innovation thrive. Of course, that doesn't mean all work relationships should be genuine. But when the right ones are, your results can be extraordinary. In fact, so can work itself. As self-help guru Anthony Robbins puts it, "Ultimately the quality of your life is the quality of your relationships." I would add this twist for work: The quality of your work relationships determines the quality of both your work and your work-life.

INVEST IN GENUINE WORK RELATIONSHIPS

None of us achieves exceptional results alone, and genuine relationships that enable exceptional results require higher commitment and investment than typical relationships. In addition to the trust-sparking essentials (go first, elevate communication, demonstrate behavioral integrity, and show up authentically), successful Trust, Inc. leaders add "build genuine relationships" to their skill set.

Investing in a relationship signals a trust-building intention. That's a powerful motivator. When someone at work, but especially a boss, wants to build a trusting and mutually beneficial relationship, it positively shifts the dynamic. Increasing the likelihood of better, stronger, and more genuine work relationships requires common-sense people-sense. Here are six uncommon ways to do that.

1. Let Your Warm-Heartedness Show

Novelist Chuck Palahniuk wrote, "The only reason why we ask other people how their weekend was is so we can tell them about our own weekend." Fortunately, most people aren't that insincere, especially those with genuine relationships. They care how your weekend was because they care about you.

However, a challenge for some bosses is how to express care, interest, and warm-heartedness at work. Too much, and objectivity or the ability to render difficult decisions may be questioned. Too little, and interactions are impersonal and aloof. The balance comes by being human. What touches you, moves you, inspires you? Show that to others. When compassion fills your heart, let it spread. When kindness fills your thoughts, act on it.

Being warm-hearted benefits the well-being and connection to you of those you're warm-hearted with, but it also helps you. Research by Professor Stephanie Brown at SUNY Stony Brook University found, "The act of experiencing compassion and helping others actually leads to tremendous mental and physical well-being for us as well. While survival of the fittest may lead to short-term gain, research clearly shows it is survival of the kindest that leads to the long-term survival of a species."[6]

It's your acts of kindness, caring, and concern that make your work relationships genuine and based on real connection. If you need a more tangible reason, "a Towers Watson study recently showed that the greatest driver of employee engagement *worldwide* is whether or not people feel their managers and organizations have genuine concern for their well-being."[7]

2. Add the Little Words

In the busyness, important little words are being forgotten—*I'm sorry*; *excuse me*; *thank you*; *you're welcome*; *please*. Take the e-mail I received from someone I didn't know asking for information on a topic from my last book. I invested half an hour answering him, providing resources, and pointing him in the right direction. When I never received an acknowledgement or thanks, I was surprised, then annoyed. When it's someone you don't know you chalk it up to rudeness; when it's someone you do, it's an action of disregard.

Now, before you label me "old-fashioned," wishing for eras gone by, consider what's communicated when we eliminate simple expressions of gratitude, appreciation, acknowledgement, or understanding, especially if we're someone's boss. Operating as if we don't "see" or care about others when we bump into them, change a commitment, or ask for or receive help reduces us to people who don't demonstrate respect, and people who take without giving. In time, those actions change who we are and the relationships we have.

Appreciation and acknowledgement are more than little words. The bottom line is, you can't have genuine relationships without politeness, recognition, or appreciation. Skipping little words isn't about having too little time—it's about having too little care. It's the way we communicate "we see what you did." If people think you didn't even notice, eventually they may not do it. In this age of digital communication and casual connections, pause and ask, are you providing enough little words to those with whom you work?

3. Give More Than You Take

Those with whom you want genuine relationships should be at the top of your give-to list. Give them answers, time, and involvement. Support their projects, development, and learning. Help them succeed. Invest personal time and energy in them.

According to Wharton Professor Adam Grant, author of *Give and Take: A Revolutionary Approach to Success*, studies show "that when helping is based on a sense of mastery and personal choice rather than duty and obligation, it's more likely to be energizing than exhausting."[8] One of the reason givers thrive, according to Grant, "comes from trust and the goodwill that they have built, but also the reputations that they create."[9]

Givers, according to Grant, are "overrepresented at the top as well as the bottom of most success metrics." If you want to be among the top, the approach to adopt is a giving style Grant calls "otherish." These people are "concerned about benefiting others, but they also keep their own interest in the rearview mirror."[10]

Of course, each relationship differs, and a giving style should be adaptive, but there's a simple rule of thumb for genuine relationship building: Give more than you take. Or, in the words of former First Lady Eleanor Roosevelt, "The most important thing in any relationship is not what you get but what you give." When you give more than you take at work, trust grows.

4. Handle Dreams With Care

It takes courage to share a dream, speak a longing, or expose a heart-desire; it can feel vulnerable sharing what may never be. Sometimes when people offer what sounds like an aspiration or goal we may not hear it as a dream. Or, if we do, we're a bit cynical of those expressing they'd like to write a book, climb Mount Everest, or start a business. More people wish and hope than act and do. And yet, it's dream power that keeps us striving and growing.

Take extra care with dreams—your own and others; never trample them. Working in a traditional corporate environment for more than two decades, it was my dream to move to the Rocky Mountains and write that often kept me going in stressful times, offered me perspective, and fueled my determination. Along the way, I occasionally shared my dream at work, and found encouraging bosses, inspiring staffs, and helpful peers.

The power in someone's dream is a reflection of who she is and where her passion lies. Her sharing is a matter of trust. When you nurture, encourage, or acknowledge someone's dream, even if it means you may lose a star on your team, you communicate to her you "see" her. We all want to be seen or known at that level. And when we're seen by someone who wants the best for us, helps us become who we're capable of becoming, and is in a genuine relationship with us, that's the person we give back to with our best work, loyalty, and trust.

Don't dismiss your own dreams or put them on the shelf either. It took 25 years to nibble my dream of living in Montana and writing, but each passing year brought forward movement. In the words of Pulitzer Prize–winning author Carl Sandburg, "Nothing happens unless first a dream." One of the aspects of a genuine relationship is leading from where and who you are. Sharing our dreams and creating a space where others can as well deepens the connection between us.

5. Think Smaller

You might have 5,000 twitter followers, 400 Facebook friends, and 300 LinkedIn professional connections, but when it comes to genuine work relationships, think small. Genuine relationships comprise an inner circle of people you count on and who count on you. They don't happen in big numbers, partly because the time and commitment needed to cultivate and nurture these relationships is significant, and partly because genuine relationships come with unspoken obligations. Although not all genuine relationships will be of the same depth, they'll have these things in common:

- You relate as individuals, not as part of a group.
- You know each other's strengths and weaknesses.
- You respect where each other is coming from—knowledge, experience, state of mind, values, beliefs.
- You appreciate each other as people, not positions.
- You have candid and confidential discussions from time to time.

Genuine relationships come with benefits. These are the people who support or naturally follow you, no matter your role, and vice versa. These are the people you may invite along from one organization or opportunity to another. And these are the people who enable you to do your own great work.

6. Hold a Value Perspective

It's not a genuine relationship unless it's mutually beneficial. How one decides what's mutually beneficial and what's not is individual. These days, 64 percent of people working in the United State are employed by companies with a hundred or more people. Commenting about these 78 million workers, columnist Jeff Greenfield positioned a challenge for leaders when he wrote, "These men and women work for someone else. And they may well have a sense that they have had a lot more to do with their boss's achievement than their boss recognizes."[11]

If you're a boss holding that perspective, don't expect to find many genuine staff relationships. For those who think the idea counts more than the execution, the vision more than the knowledge to turn it into a reality, the design more than the development, the brand marketing more than customer service, or the leader more than the follower, think again. Trust, Inc. leaders understand one doesn't happen without the other. Genuine relationships thrive when people hold a value perspective, and each person is valued for what he or she brings and contributes to the bigger whole. It's understanding *you* couldn't do what you do without them, and vice versa.

GROWTH COMES THROUGH RELATIONSHIPS

Twentieth-century novelist Sarah Grand wrote, "Our opinion of people depends less upon what we see in them, than upon what they make us see in ourselves." Our relationships, especially genuine ones, help us develop and grow. They offer a mirror, helping us see aspects of ourselves we might not otherwise encounter. Psychological studies have confirmed that these relationships help us understand and strengthen who we are. Here are three ways:

1. They provide "a context for sensemaking about how a person creates value in a given context."

2. They "strengthen a person's resolve to confront challenges to authenticity with moral courage."

3. They offer an opportunity "to trust that positive and negative feedback is accurate and well-intended."[12]

Barbara Fredrickson, professor of psychology at the University of North Carolina, offers additional insight into the personal benefit of these trusting relationships in her research on the science of emotions. According to Dr. Fredrickson, positive emotions impact our personal growth "first by opening you up: your outlook quite literally expands."[13]

Not only do positive emotions, such as trust, increase the amount of the hormone oxytocin circulating through our brain and body, but they also help us tune in more to others and nudge our connections. These positive emotions even mold us. "In fact," said Dr. Fredrickson, "my research and that of others shows that positive emotions can set off upward spirals in your life, self-sustaining trajectories of growth that lift you up to become a better version of yourself."[14]

Genuine relationships bring us these positive emotions. They help us see through others' eyes what we may be blind to about ourselves, and reflect to us our best-self characteristics, gifts, and talents. The ability to hear and learn about ourselves in a trusting and genuine relationship expedites self-discovery and personal growth. How have your genuine work relationships created more self-knowledge for you? How do they contribute to your success?

REFLECTIVE THINKING
Learning From Others

If a specific question doesn't apply to you, let it spark your thinking or curiosity about genuine relationships. Consider writing your answers to increase personal insights.

1. Think of a few genuine work relationships you have. Consider each. What has working with that person taught you about yourself, positively or negatively?

2. How have you changed or grown through trusting work relationships? Non-trusting ones?

3. Sometimes feedback about ourselves can be difficult to hear. What feedback about you was difficult? Was it the feedback or the person giving it that made it that way? Why?

4. Do you think your boss "sees you" as the person you are? What about your staff? Why or why not?

5. Whom would you want to thank for providing you greater self-awareness during the process of working with him or her? What did he or she do that enabled your self-learning?

> 6. Is there anything stopping you from building genuine relationships at work?
>
> 7. In what ways do you help others see their best self in action, or gain greater self-awareness? How can you do more of this for others?

Another benefit of genuine relationships was captured by a 19th-century British Prime Minister, Benjamin Disraeli, when he said, "The greatest good you can do for another is not just share your riches, but reveal to them their own." That's what trusting, genuine relationships do. When we learn from each other, grow as a result of our interactions, and become better known to each other, we discover what we're capable of and how to better bring our talents to our work.

AN "UNSUPPORTED PERSONALITY"

For many, a genuine relationship with self is harder than a genuine relationship with others. The ability to show up and do great work starts with self, but it's not easy—at least it hasn't been for me. Technical savvy is not among my natural traits, so when attempts at using a wireless printer continued to fail, I was gratified when I enticed the printer to print. Expectantly, I went to retrieve the queued pages, only to discover just one sheet in the tray. The error message on that page read: "Unsupported Personality."

That could have been an error message about my life. Don't get me wrong, I've had support and love from family and friends my entire life. The "unsupported personality" part is me-to-me. I have an inconsistent, often unsupportive relationship with myself. Sometimes I like me—sometimes I don't. Sometimes I'm happy with what I've done and who I am, only to be disappointed and discouraged when I don't live up to expectations of what I think I should've accomplished, or when I fall short of the person I think I should or could be. Sometimes I'm self-encouraging, other times self-sabotaging.

That error message got me thinking: If someone treated me the way I've treated myself, I'd consider her more an enemy than a friend. I'd see her professed love as conditional, expectations self-fulfilling, and intentions untrustworthy. I'd easily recognize that her controlling, limiting, and fear-inciting methods were not in my best interests, and I'd distance myself from her and look for better relationships. As my mother used to remind me, I can at times be my own worst enemy.

I know I'm not alone. I hear similar things from colleagues and people I mentor. Many of you may find it easier to be a friend to someone else than to yourself, to be in a genuine, caring, and trusting relationship with others than with yourself, and forgive everyone but yourself. Yet, how can you offer the best of who you are to the world if you're not offering the best of who you are to you?

We need a *supported* personality—a genuine trusting *self-*relationship—in order to unlock our life's music. We need to develop, nurture, and grow these self-relationships as much as any others, so we can bring our gifts to the world and do the great work we're capable of doing.

PART III

BEYOND TRUST, INC.—THE CHALLENGE OF TRUST

We do not have to become heroes overnight. Just a step at a time, meeting each thing that comes up, seeing it is not as dreadful as it appeared, discovering we have the strength to stare it down.

~ Eleanor Roosevelt

CHAPTER 11

Stumbling Blocks and Other Realities

Make the best use of what is in your power, and take the rest as it happens.

~ Epictetus

The room was filled with second-shift coal miners required to attend training. Topics included Fire Suppression, Fire Safety, Safety through Wellness, and Substance Abuse. The topic I'd been hired to present wasn't on the agenda, but word of mouth had spread through crossed-armed groups that the mystery topic was *about trust.*

As if a vow of silence had been sworn, the body language of the all-male audience confirmed what I'd been briefed on: Trust, or rather its lack, was a "big issue" at the mine. A long history of nasty contract negotiations, name-calling, and strike threats resulted in the current situation of distrust, lack of respect, minimal interaction, and finger-pointing. Despite sessions involving hundreds of employees, only one question was asked the entire week: "Why doesn't management have to come to these trust classes?" They did, but the rumor mill claimed otherwise. Beyond that, the silence held in each session. Yet by week's end, several men had privately sought me out to ask a question, explain an issue, or offer a comment. A few wanted help with distrust spillover into their rural town. As one miner explained, "Our kids used to play together, but no more."

Hopefully you'll never have to deal with trust this broken in your Trust, Inc., but the reality is authentic trust can be betrayed. This chapter addresses the when and how of rebuilding trust, plus potholes and stumbling blocks including unsupportive bosses and distrusting work cultures. It also offers tips for nurturing a trust culture throughout the ebb and flow of relationships and organizational change.

BROKEN TRUST

The law in ancient Rome required the engineer who built an arch to be the first to stand beneath it. Perhaps if the impact of our actions were as publicly visible and as instantly understandable, we wouldn't be facing diminishing trust levels in most workplaces. The unspoken toll of broken trust impacts productivity, engagement, creativity, effort, and a shared economy. It affects well-being, relationships, and optimism, changing how we view and embrace our work.

According to Dennis S. Reina and Michelle L. Reina, trust researchers and coauthors of *Trust and Betrayal in the Workplace*, "nine of every 10 employees experience some kind of breach of trust in the workplace on a regular basis. When trust erodes, morale declines, performance plummets, and employees become disengaged and leave."[1]

Sometimes we make mistakes, or things don't work out, or matters outside our control cause commitments not to be honored. But sometimes we break promises, or say one thing and do another.

Disappointment? Yes. Diminished trust? Maybe. Irreparable damage? Sometimes. There are minor and major trust-breaches, intentional and unintentional trust-breaking, and differences in what's required for repair.

On a positive note, Wharton Professor Maurice E. Schweitzer and his colleagues discovered that "trust harmed by untrustworthy behavior can be effectively restored when individuals observe a consistent series of trustworthy actions."[2]

However, what happens if we never planned to honor our commitments? What then? Of all the behaviors negatively affecting trust at work, lying tops the list of what people say when they think of trust betrayed. As Dr. Schweitzer found, "Trust harmed by the same untrustworthy actions *and deception*, never fully recovers—even when deceived participants receive a promise, an apology, and observe a consistent series of trustworthy actions." Bottom line? "Deception causes enduring harm to trust."[3]

Long-term distrust can change a safe and secure environment to one of fear and trepidation. According to University of British Columbia Professor Sandra L. Robinson, "Turning things around from distrust is really hard because everything is viewed through the lens of distrust." In fact, "the distrust problem" is something researchers don't fully understand, Robinson says.[4] But they do know distrust can linger and have a significantly negative impact.

Although you can't change the overall workplace trust trajectory or the actions of others, you can change your own. Typically, you can rebuild authentic trust, repair trust-damaging potholes, and address trust's stumbling blocks in your trust-pocket. You can lead through these challenges.

Rebuilding Authentic Trust

Fortunately, most people aren't involved in deliberate deceptions at work. Most leaders don't intentionally lie, manipulate, or deceive those they lead. Most want thriving work cultures. Authentic trust develops through critical thought and experience, with accountability at its core, and *can* be regained. If there wasn't a possibility it could be rebuilt after being broken, it wouldn't be authentic trust.

Because relationships matter to those who give authentic trust, repairing trust is a priority. When there isn't deception or significant trust betrayal, you can regain authentic trust using these practical approaches:

- **Be like the Roman engineer.** Whatever your work, operate as if you must publicly stand for your results. This includes acknowledging trust breaks. Research is mixed on whether an apology and expression of remorse significantly enables rebuilding trust at work, but researchers have found "a promise helped initial trust recovery" because it signals a positive intention of behavior change.[5] Long-term trust recovery, however, requires the observation of *consistent* trustworthy behaviors.

- **Own your role in what happened.** We make mistakes, hurt people unintentionally, and sometimes, despite our good intentions, things still don't work out or consequences linger. You create opportunity for trust restoration when you accept you're a responsible driver culpable for missteps, not a passenger along for the ride. Own what's yours. Whether you broke the trust, responded poorly when someone else did, or perpetuated distrust, relationships by their very nature are two-sided. What did you contribute to the current state of distrust?

- **Facilitate discovery and resolution.** Elevated communication with honest dialogue is essential and may require a neutral facilitator to begin the process. The goal is to understand what happened, why it happened, the impact on the parties involved, and the next small step in relationship rebuilding. Sometimes diminished trust results from misunderstandings, miscommunications, or misassumptions. Address these quickly. If you allow trust-related issues to fester, the resolution process can be challenging. Success depends on mutual desire, active openness, deep listening, clarity of intention, withholding judgment, and a non-defensive style. It's akin to any good conflict-resolution approach.

- **Assess your beliefs.** Are you quick to forgive or long to remember? Do you believe people can change, or that character is fixed? Beliefs impact your ability to rebuild trust. Researchers from the University of Wisconsin found, "Individuals who believe that moral character can change over time are more likely to trust following an apology and trustworthy behavior than are individuals who believe that moral character cannot change." In fact, including a message about people's general ability to change made a positive difference in the trust-recovery process.[6]

- **Heighten self-awareness.** Were you aware of trust diminishing, or were you surprised? Are you operating from good intentions or manipulative self-interests? Are you honoring commitments and fulfilling promises? The power of behavioral integrity can't be overstated when rebuilding trust. How will people perceive your actions from this point on? Heightened self-awareness is required. Don't provide any reason for someone to doubt your trustworthiness or intentions.

- **Restart trust.** "To trust someone is to act as if they are trustworthy," according to Solomon and Flores.[7] Treating trust as a verb does that. The question isn't, "Do I have trust here?" but rather, "Am I creating trust here?" You restart trust with the small act of giving a little trust. As hard as that can be when trust is betrayed or becomes distrust, someone must go first, regardless of who was at fault. If the relationship is worth rebuilding, your willingness and openness to signal that it is makes a difference to the outcome. The same dimmer-switch approach to trust building can be used for trust-rebuilding. But before you write me off as a Pollyanna, let me be clear: It won't always work. Not all relationships that mattered can be trusted ones again, nor can all broken trust be repaired.

- **Give it time.** It takes time to regain what was. Be patient. People react differently to the same trust transgression. Some forgive quickly; others carry anger baggage for years. The self-healing benefits of forgiveness are well documented. Where are you on the forgiveness continuum if trust is broken? As authors Solomon and Flores wrote, "The real danger is not only losing trust, it is giving up on trust." They note two essentials for trust restoration: "the mood of hope and the complex act of forgiving."[8] If the relationship still matters, keep trying.

- **Tell the right stories.** We all have stories about broken trust at work. But these aren't the stories you need to tell. In an era of distrust, share stories of trust *rebuilt*. Storytelling is a choice—you can plant story weeds, adding toxins to the work culture, fueling dark-side politics, and enhancing silo thinking, or you can plant story seeds of trust rebuilt, relationships renewed, work enhanced by honest dialogue and openness, and positive actions taken. The stories you tell about trust built or trust broken are critical stories illustrating to those you lead not only what you believe, but also what you're open to building. In the words of Dr. Pamela Rutledge, director of the Media Psychology Research Center, "Stories are how we explain how things work, how we make decisions, how we justify our decisions, how we persuade others, how we understand our place in the world, create our identities, and define and teach social values."[9] Stories are most telling about the teller. What kind of stories are you telling?

WHEN THE TRUST, INC. PATH HAS POTHOLES

Don't expect to build your trust-pocket without falling into a few potholes. The following questions and answers address common holes lurking on the path to work trust and ways to maneuver around them. You'll find more in a reader download called "Seven Common Trust, Inc. Derailers, Potholes, and Mistakes" (see the Resources at the end of the book).

1. How Can I Create a Trust, Inc. if the Company Culture Is One of Distrust?

No one needs permission to create a trust-pocket. Nor do you need alignment with an existing company culture. Look around. There are plenty of subcultures where you work—some great, some not. The leader influences the subculture. Since trust is a local issue, what's essential is aligning your Trust, Inc. with organizational priorities and strategies: You'll have difficulty creating a trust-culture within any organization if you're not supporting its mission, objectives, and goals. Take your organizational culture's strengths, values, and initiatives and overlay your operating style of authentic trust.

Trust, Inc. isn't *what* you do, it's *how* you do it. Culture isn't a *what*, it's a *how*. The key in managing a successful Trust, Inc. is understanding you'll only succeed if you deliver the results that matter to the bigger organization. Results are the tangible measure of success in most companies. You're first measured on *what* you do. Your leadership style dictates the how. Being a leader who operates with authentic trust is a style that gets results; it's not the result you're trying to get.

2. My Boss Doesn't Buy "Soft Stuff" or the Need for Engagement or Transparency. What Can I Do?

Don't try to convince your boss that operating with trust makes good business sense. Show him. Don't argue the business merits of engagement, innovation, and greater accountability. Show him. And don't attempt to change his thinking. It doesn't matter what he thinks about trust. It only matters what *you* do with it.

One of your roles is to make your boss look good. Do that and you won't get pushback. Turn in exemplary results, and you won't get "soft stuff" grief. Reduce turnover, lower costs, and exceed expectations and you won't need to do any other convincing.

The reality is your boss doesn't care if you have a Trust, Inc. He cares if you hit your target, exceed your objectives, and create business solutions. One of the common ways organizational cultures change is from grassroots success. When you get great results, others will notice, want to discover how you're doing it, and opt to model your approach.

3. What Should I Share About My Trust, Inc.?

The mistake many leaders make is talking about what they're *going* to do, what they *want* to achieve, how they're seeking permission to do something, or how they want others to come onboard. Those who lead a thriving Trust, Inc. know its action that changes opinions in time, not words. If down the road that doesn't happen, you may want to revisit the kind of company you want to work in.

You don't need to talk about showing up authentically, elevating communication, or going first in giving trust—just do it. When your team consistently delivers great work and the best candidates want to join you, people notice. When those you lead consistently come through when others don't, people notice. And when your Trust, Inc. is full of engaged, energized, and innovative people, the word will spread.

4. Because Trust Is at an All-Time Low, Won't That Affect My Ability to Create a Trust, Inc.?

Not unless you let it. How you give, create, build, and nurture authentic trust doesn't depend on what people think is happening "out there." They're focused "in here"—with their work group, boss, or situation. Don't let headlines or Gallup polls become self-fulfilling expectations. Don't let peers who believe others are untrustworthy influence you. And don't let herd mentality dictate how you choose to lead.

People want to trust you, even in an era of distrust. Give them reason and they likely will. The science behind what makes us trust or not offers this reality: We need connection and want to trust. Typically, trust is part of our everyday lives. We drop our child at daycare, buy a new product, or share information with the person next to us. But just because we're wired to trust doesn't mean we're always good at building trust.

According to social psychologist Roderick M. Kramer, professor at Stanford Graduate School of Business, "Some of the social signals we send are too subtle, though we don't realize it. Most of us tend to underinvest in communicating our trustworthiness to others, because we take it for granted that they know or can readily discern our wonderful qualities of fairness, honesty, and integrity."[10] You increase your trust-building odds by sending "loud, clear, and consistent signals" according to Kramer.

5. Isn't Giving Trust First Just Semantics and Another Way of Saying "Trust, But Verify?"

No. The phrase President Reagan made popular, "trust, but verify," is a common pushback from those who believe people need to earn trust. Despite this common thought, people can't earn your authentic trust. People who insist others must prove trustworthiness spark distrust, not trust. That belief aligns with a Theory X philosophy that people inherently can't be trusted. Hence, they must prove it to you. Just as trust begets trust, distrust begets distrust.

When you operate with trust as a verb, giving it first, you invest in the other person. Withholding trust until you decide someone proves she's worthy, or "earned it," communicates the opposite. It makes the outcome more important than the relationship. Of course, sometimes outcome *should* be the priority: When President Reagan used the phrase "trust, but verify" during the Cold War, it referred to information reliability and increased transparency related to nuclear arsenals.[11] In that case, outcome definitely trumped relationship. That's not true in trust-pockets.

6. When Business Is Bad, the Increased Pressure and Intensity Can Cripple Teams. How Will Trust, Inc. Fare?

That depends on you. How will you handle it when budgets are cut, layoffs are required, or favorite projects are eliminated? Will you communicate more, or less? Will you become controlling, or lead through the challenges? These are the times that make or break bosses. When everyone is watching, what will you do?

Many people change their behavior when pressure mounts, decisions become difficult, or company politics push them beyond common sense. However, those leaders continuing to operate as someone worthy of their staff's trust will be rewarded with greater commitment, loyalty, efforts, and involvement.

During difficult times, make things easier, not harder for your staff. Increase lines of communication, and help them transition from change. Dispel rumors, shield pressures, and increase your kindness and consideration. These are the times people will remember how you showed up and who you *really* were when it mattered.

7. What Are Some Other Potholes I Might Expect?

There are small and large potholes and stumbling blocks along the way to a thriving, sustainable Trust, Inc. Anticipating them offers the strategic advantage of being more prepared. Here are a few.

Expect the Unexpected
✓ Don't think your words are ever "off the record" or totally confidential. Be prepared: anything you say or do may come back at you.
✓ At some point, you'll have staff that disappoints you, violates your trust, or undermines your authority. How you respond will set the tone for others.
✓ Not everyone wants you to succeed. That can include staff, a boss, or peers. Don't be naïve to company politics.
✓ We all have blind spots. Find people you can trust who will help you see yours.
✓ Good bosses are given a little leeway, but the operative word is *little*. Always take your own words seriously.
✓ Don't wait for a crisis. Develop safety nets, support structures, and genuine relationships before you need them.
✓ People will negatively attribute things to you that aren't your doing, holding you accountable. Without blaming others or the situation, learn from it and move on.

✓ Ignoring people problems is a big trust sinkhole. Don't let them envelop you. Address the situations that need addressing clearly, firmly, and quickly.

✓ To be a Trust, Inc. leader when others aren't can be a lonely path. Have trusted allies outside of work to lean on, bounce ideas off of, collaborate with, and learn from.

How will you show up in these situations—with openness and trust or detachment and control? How will others see your behavior—trust-enhancing or trust-diminishing? The way to handle the unexpected well is to stay grounded in best-self behaviors.

REFLECTIVE EXERCISE
Avoiding Trust Potholes

Mark the statements that are more true than false for you, most of the time, at work.

1. I take extra care of myself during stressful and difficult work times, knowing I best help others by first helping myself.

2. I can let things go and get on with moving forward emotionally even in challenging times at work.

3. When relationships are strained or trust is damaged, I quickly work to repair things.

4. I'm comfortable dealing with conflict or addressing morale issues with my staff.

5. I'm willing to admit when I'm wrong or in over my head, and I ask for help when needed.

6. I encourage feedback when my staff thinks my words and actions don't match up.

7. Part of my job is damage control—setting the record straight, telling the truth, and offering insights about what's going on.

8. I need to buffer stress, and provide support and help to my team so that organizational turmoil and change don't overpower or encompass us.

9. Talking about trust, and what that looks like, is a regular approach I take with my team.

10. I consider myself the catalyst for creating a Trust, Inc., but everyone contributes to making our culture a thriving one.

Self-discovery: Give yourself one point for each number circled. With a score of 8 or more, you can feel confident your leadership approach can help maneuver your Trust, Inc. through challenges.

NURTURING YOUR TRUST, INC. CULTURE

Leading a thriving trust-pocket, with consistently great results from engaged and energized people, requires dealing with the ebb and flow of relationships, nurturing the culture, addressing problems, managing conflict, and handling stumbling blocks. Here are three of my favorite ways to do that:

❖ **Use your ingredients.** Anyone who knows me knows I'm not into cooking. But I know a good relationship is like a good casserole—only those who create it know what's in it. You and I will have different ingredients in our trust-cultures. My three essential ingredients include:

- Every day recommitment and persistence; tending the culture is a priority.

- Make it purposeful; work to make a difference; re-member the whys.

- Help others bloom. Make it safe for people to be who they are.

❖ **Protect your nest.** Be like the mother robin outside my of-fice window and defend your eggs against trust-opponents—naysayers, rumors, bureaucracy, inflexibility, mediocrity, mi-cromanaging, blaming, and inconsistency. The golden eggs to hatch from your nest include everything from exceptional results and high performance to innovative solutions and un-imagined possibilities. There's much at stake in your nest—protect, feed, and nurture it. You'll need to be as diligent and fierce as that mother bird to keep trust-nibblers away.

❖ **Don't play it safe.** Too often managers use the "If it ain't broke, don't fix it" strategy, lounging in a status quo of okay-ness, or not wanting to rock the boat. But effective leaders don't lounge. They contribute. And they don't play it safe. They play it smart. That requires a bit of soul-courage from time to time. People follow people who know what they're *for* and are willing to work to bring it into existence.

There's a story about Phidias, a Greek sculptor working on the Acropolis: As he was finishing a statue of Athena, which would stand a hundred feet high next to a marble wall, an onlooker asked, "Why are you chiseling strands of hair on the back of her head where no one will see them or even know they're there?" Phidias replied, "I'll know."

It's the same with Trust, Inc. leaders. You'll know if you're giv-ing and nurturing trust. You'll know if you're maneuvering around potholes or are swallowed by them. You'll know if you're contribut-ing and making a difference at work or not. As news anchor Brian Williams remarked in his George Washington University commence-ment speech, "You don't actually have to build a rocket or go into space, but please take us somewhere. Please keep us moving. Push us, lift us up. Make us better."

Please do. Don't get stuck in potholes, lost on stumbling blocks, or daunted by setbacks. They'll actually make you stronger by building your character, wisdom, and strength to do so much more.

CHAPTER 12

The Courage to Trust

Every accomplishment starts with the decision to try.
~ Gail Devers

It's strange what lobsters do when a wave strands them on rocks. Instead of crawling forward just a few feet to reach the water, they remain where they are. Most die waiting for the ocean to come to them instead of trying to get back to it.

Most people wait too. They wait for an organizational initiative to improve a deteriorating culture; wait for HR to do an opinion survey or sound an alarm; wait for a boss to notice the challenge they're dealing with; wait until distrust impacts the bottom line so someone will finally do something.

Like the lobster, many don't try to reach a self-sustaining environment. They die waiting—not literally, of course, but their work passion, initiative, commitment, and motivation perish in the process. The lobster's instinct is to stay in the rocks, and typically ours is too. Why rock the boat? Why navigate a trust-building sea of uncertainty? Why chance a public failure, lone venture, or unsupported endeavor to build a trust-pocket against the rising tide of cynicism and distrust? Why not stay safely hidden?

One thing is certain: If you don't move forward *toward trust*, despite fear or trepidation, you'll risk lingering in a sea of mediocrity with reduced influence and results. We risk a future of work cultures that spark passion, engagement, and innovation if we collectively stay on the rocks, accepting as inevitable the state of workplace trust today. Of course, understanding the importance of work trust and building it are quite different. As novelist Caleb Carr said, "It is the greatest truth of our age: Information is not knowledge." This book is information; knowledge is what you'll have after venturing beyond the rocks.

Sure, a workplace-culture wave may arrive, but don't count on it. One thing the Great Recession clarified is that ultimately you're in charge of your work future. What do you want it to be? How do you want to lead? What difference do you want to make?

There are three acts of courage related to a thriving Trust, Inc. that'll keep you swimming forward in a sea of opportunity. That's what this chapter is about. Consider it a call to action for a better work future for you and those you lead. It only takes a few venturing from the rocks of discouragement, disengagement, and distrust to show others a better way—the focus of local trust any leader, anywhere can do. But, a bit of courage is needed to get us off the rocks.

The reality is, whether or not you build a trust-pocket, trust others, elevate communication, build genuine relationships, or authentically show up, you'll get battered around from time to time. Life is like that. Conflicts, difficulties, setbacks, and negative events are inevitable, but what isn't is how you'll handle what comes your way.

ACTS OF COURAGE AT WORK

Being a leader doesn't give you courage or make you fearless. However, it provides greater reason to act despite your fear. As James Neil Hollingsworth penned under pseudonym Ambrose Redmoon, "Courage is not the absence of fear, but rather the judgment that something else is more important than fear." What's important to you?

Bill Treasurer, author of *Courage Goes to Work*, talks about workplace courage this way: "When you're anxious, worried, or scared and feel the urge to hunker down and play it safe, that's the time you need to do just the opposite. Playing it safe never leads to greatness. That's where courage comes in."[1]

Trusting when you're hesitant takes courage. Trusting again despite career setbacks or failure takes courage. Rebuilding trust that can be broken again takes courage. Speaking up when others won't takes courage. Being authentic, showing vulnerability, and walking *your* talk takes courage. Making the difficult but right decisions takes courage. So does building a thriving trust-pocket in a culture of distrust.

Trusting Again After Career Setback or Job Loss

When I didn't get a big promotion I expected, it took courage to weather the disappointment among company politics and rumors. It took courage to accept a minimum-wage position to pay the bills—a position friends told me was "beneath" me—after I was fired from my first professional job. Broken trust can break your spirit, impale your emotional well-being, and scar your heart. If I hadn't trusted again—both self-trust and trusting others—the learning from these experiences wouldn't have offered me the stepping stones and opportunities to create a successful future.

Harboring mistrust and anger over broken promises, career setbacks, or job loss can limit you as easily as a 3-foot wall traps an impala: This animal is able to jump 10 feet high, covering distances of more than 30 feet, but it won't jump unless it can see where its feet will land. If you won't trust again unless you know your trust won't be betrayed; won't risk until you know it's risk-proof; won't step out to offer your talents unless you're sure it's safe—you create a self-limiting enclosure. Stepping again toward trust requires courage.

Moving Forward

❖ **Shed anger.** How does blaming the company or its leaders help *you*? How will holding on to anger and distrust bring you closer to the future you want? As long as anger weighs you down, your past blocks your future. Elizabeth Kenney, an early 20th-century nurse-advocate for physical therapy, said, "He who angers you conquers you." We give power to those who hurt us when we cling to our pain. Don't waste emotional well-being blaming others. To move forward, you must shed the anger and hurt. A helpful resource is Dr. Fred Luskin's book, *Forgive for Good*.

❖ **Leverage currency.** People hire, promote, and want to work with those whom they know and trust, or whom someone they trust knows and trusts. Leverage your trust currency to find a new position, boss, or team. Who trusts you? Whom do they trust? Genuine relationships offer you the most trust to leverage. Tap them when faced with job loss or career setback—*and* be sure to return the favor.

❖ **Restore self-trust.** Damaged self-trust from a "life happens" event such as losing your job can be a precursor to distrusting others. Self-trust is shaken by this experience. The most important relationship you have is with yourself. Start there. Strengthen that relationship by doing the inner work needed to build back lost self-trust. As Ralph Waldo Emerson reminds, "Self-trust is the first secret to success." Once you can trust yourself again, you can begin to trust others.

❖ **Choose to give.** Trusting again doesn't happen because you want it to happen, or when others are "good enough," "dependable enough," or "trustworthy enough" for them to earn back your trust. Giving trust is a choice, decision, or judgment you make when you put confidence in or rely on someone else. You'll only regain trust when you have the courage to give it again.

It's true that giving authentic trust comes with the possibility of being broken, but so what? Loving comes with the possibility of heartbreak, but not loving or trusting diminishes relationships, results, and your *life*. Don't allow career setbacks and the resulting distrust to hijack your future well-being, or hinder you from building the trusting relationships and trust-pocket you need for your success.

Finding (and Using) Your Voice at Work

Focusing on what you want more of, being willing to speak *for* or work *for* that, is what it means to find and use your voice at work. A type of soul courage is required. Whether it's having courage to say no when you'd be more popular if you said yes, giving difficult feedback, eliminating poor-performing staff, or working to bring transforming change, those who build trust currency in the new workplace lend their voices toward creating *positive* environments where people can show up and do great work—places where everyone can be winning at working.

Often, this is the opposite of what we're used to. We're used to people telling us the things that are wrong, that need changing, or that they're against. But using your voice isn't about working against something; it's about working toward something—focusing on what you want more of, not less of; what you want to bring about or make better.

Nobel Prize–winner and humanitarian Mother Teresa offered an illustration of the concept in an often quoted interpretation of her words: "I was once asked why I don't participate in anti-war demonstrations. I said that I will never do that, but as soon as you have a pro-peace rally, I'll be there."[2] The difference in personal commitment involved in being *for* something rather than *against* something is palpable. Focus on what you'll help bring into existence. Successful leaders do that.

Trust, Inc. Leaders Use Their Voices to...
✓ Talk about trust, not distrust.
✓ Build authentic trust, not diminish it.
✓ Champion the right things to do, not rail against mistakes or assign blame.
✓ Promote the ideas, talents, and contributions of those they work with, not take undue credit.
✓ Give ideas and information away to help the greater good, not competitively hoard them.
✓ Help people transition from change, not leave people stuck in the past.
✓ Provide others with opportunities to excel, not ways to make them stumble.
✓ Manage to the trustworthy vast majority doing a great job, not the small percentage who aren't.
✓ Focus on what people can do, not what they can't.

✓ Bring about a work culture in which everyone can be winning, not where just a few win.
✓ Embrace the individual, not apply stereotypes by generation, ethnicity, or gender.
✓ Build understanding, inclusion, and well-being, not division, exclusion, and unhealthy conflict.
✓ Keep raising the bar to excellence, not settle for mediocrity.
✓ Give back to a larger world, not stay in a self-centered one.
✓ Make a bigger difference for others, not a bigger difference for self.

"Finding" your voice is actually an inaccurate thought. Your voice, that inner knowing and connection to what matters to you, isn't lost—it's quieted. When your mind is still, you'll hear it. The problem at work is we're not as quiet, thoughtful, or reflective as often as we're reactive, overworked, and responsive. If you want to increase "finding" and using your voice at work you'll need to practice.

Listen for Your Voice

❖ **Focus on wants.** Turn thoughts of what you don't want into a vision of what you do want. If you want trust, focus on trust, not control; focus on teamwork, not silos; accountability, not excuses; strengths, not weaknesses; results, not blame; well-being, not stress. As you reframe negative "don't wants" into positive "wants," listen carefully. Within your positive wants and thoughts, you'll hear your voice.

❖ **Give what's missing.** As the Chinese proverb reminds, "Better to light a candle than curse the darkness." Every time you curse the darkness, notice the light that's missing. Are you missing unbiased thinking, openness, integrity? Give it. Are you missing compassion or genuine connection? Accountability, authenticity, or tolerance? Passion or commitment? Be the person who gives what's missing, or speaks up for it, and you'll hear your voice in the giving.

❖ **Play from where you are.** There's a story about legendary golfer Bobby Jones responding to a question about his health: "It's not going to get better, it's going to get worse all the time. But don't fret. Remember, we play the ball where it lies." When a challenge is difficult or circumstances overwhelming, it's an opportunity to hear your voice. When you discover insights, knowledge, skills, and perspectives enabling you to play from where you are with the best of who you are, listen.

Using your voice at work is like the Karma Kitchen restaurant, "where your bill always reads $0 because the meal is a gift from people who came before you, and you are invited to pay it forward for those who come after."[3] When you work to bring about what's positive and helpful, and contribute to the greater good, you're creating the equivalent "gift"—a thriving trust-culture for those who come after you. You're helping to show what *can be*. You're teaching future Trust, Inc. leaders how they can lead with trust, enabling others to bring their contributions to the world. You're creating a better present *and* paying it forward.

Being a Trust-Creator in an Era of Distrust

It can be lonely to travel a path others aren't on, as well as difficult, scary, or confusing. The peer pressure to maintain an "us"-versus-"them" mentality, remain a disgruntled staff member, or operate with reciprocal dark-side politics can hold some people back. Lack of support from a disinterested or untrustworthy boss can increase the challenge. And cynical, disengaged, or myopic staff can make you wonder, "Why am I even trying?"

Being able to counter these pulls is one of the biggest hurdles you'll face as a Trust, Inc. leader. Work doesn't happen in a vacuum. What can you *really* do if you're swimming against a culture tide? The first question should be, what are you *willing* to do?

REFLECTIVE EXERCISE
Are You Willing and Able?

Choose one answer for each statement below, assigning points accordingly.

1 = Able, but not willing; 2 = Willing, but not able; 3 = Both willing and able.

Total your points.

1. When it comes to trust-building, I'll step up and give trust first—at least to those I lead.

2. If the trust I give is broken and the relationship still matters, I'll work to rebuild it.

3. I'll persist in doing the right thing, even when others disagree with me.

4. Typically, I follow my boss's direction, and having a good relationship with him matters to me, but I'll push back on issues I feel strongly about.

5. I'll fight for my staff to get the increases, recognition, and rewards they deserve.

6. When politics are rampant and impact my team, I'll refrain from responding in kind to the darker antics others use.

7. I won't look for permission to create a trust-pocket; I'll just do it.

8. My role as a leader is to help others succeed, and through them the organization. To do that well, I need to create an emotionally safe environment for those I lead.

9. I'll use my voice to actively work toward what I want more of, advocating for positive culture transformation.

10. I can start small and work toward my own trust-pocket one step at a time, no matter the current organizational culture or direction.

Self-Scoring: If you scored 14–22, you're more willing than currently able to progress against organizational tides. You may find it helpful to review tips in Chapters 1–5. If you scored 23–30, feel confident your self-confidence will assist your results. You may find it useful to review tips in Chapters 6–10 to maintain your grounding if the tide shifts. If you scored less than 14, now may be a good time to refocus your leadership goals.

You can find reasons to stay snuggly on the rocks. You can find reasons not to do something out of your comfort zone. The job of test pilot in the 1940s was to "push the envelope" of a plane's performance beyond the standard specs of speed, distance, and altitude, trying to make planes go faster, farther, or higher. As a leader, your job is to push the envelope too—to create ways for your team to go faster, farther, or higher. To do that, you'll need plenty of trust currency and a winning culture founded on authentic trust. You will need the same pioneering spirit and courage as those test pilots.

Courage Essentials for Trust, Inc. Leaders

- **The courage to persist.** In a work world addicted to instant results, messaging, and information, having the patience, fortitude, and persistence to hold the course for the long term requires vision, confidence, and an ability to enable sustainable results rather than fleeting, short-term results.

- **The courage to think independently.** It's easier to follow the herd toward the latest bandwagon solutions or headline-topping approaches. But complex problems of distrust, disengagement, and tethered passions won't be solved that way. Trust is sparked by *you*, not by a program.

- **The courage to revisit trust.** Authentic trust doesn't sit on a shelf waiting to be used. It fluctuates through actions taken and relationships nurtured. It requires self-awareness to understand the consequences of actions, whether they're well-intentioned or not. Monitoring and revisiting trust-making, -building, and -restoring is essential.

- **The courage to lead.** There's much written on the topic of leadership, and an equal or greater amount on management. But here's what great leaders know: You're more dependent on those you lead than they are on you. Real leadership, the kind that inspires natural followership, doesn't come from a position or title; it comes from who you are, and how you do what you do.

Rewards from having the courage to trust can be small, medium, and large—everything from impacting individual lives to finding transformational relationships, and from better results to better workplaces. Here's what I know to be true: *The courage to trust is really about the courage to live, in the deepest sense.* Without trust we swim on the surface of our relationships, languishing in the shallow end. With trust, we can dive deeply together to explore, discover, innovate, and become who we are capable of becoming.

YOUR TRUST-LEGACY

A hundred people I didn't know gathered on the top floor of a New York City hotel. A few sought fame or fortune, but most were there undertaking an endeavor with the hope of making a difference, sharing their story to help others, or bringing awareness to people in need.

I sought the back of the room, nearest the exit sign, choosing a seat on the aisle. Where I sat mattered to me so much that I'd deliberately arrived early to choose my place, recognizing this quirky aisle-sitting obsession as a part of me. As a child, having a fire destroy our home in the middle of the night shaped that aisle preference as certainly as my mother's DNA shaped my face. Being sick as a young woman, experiencing a failed first marriage, being fired from my first professional job, and losing my father to Alzheimer's also shaped me. So did growing up in a time of bomb shelters, war protests, and glass ceilings, and being married 38 years to my best friend, experiencing the joys and challenges of motherhood and grandmother-hood, and traveling in Africa.

Yet, I haven't thought of life's occurrences and influences in quite the same way since that New York event. It was there I met a woman who had lost her college-age son to suicide, and was now devoting her life to warning others of the signs. I met a survivor of street brutality dedicating his life to rescuing troubled teens; an accident victim told he'd never walk who just ran his first 10K; and a man who lost 250 pounds, clawing his way out of depression to help others defeat their demons and restore their health. These people became who they are through their life's experiences, and so do each of us.

Every headline and book read, every person met, an every experience had or heard about—good or not good—finds its way into how we think, what we believe, what we don't believe, and who we trust or don't trust. Similar to constantly re-forming DNA, they shape who we become.

How different would you or I be in another time or place, with different life circumstances, work experiences, or people around us?

How much of who we are is a result of whom we've known, where we've lived or worked, and whom we've met or not met? Yet, we're shapers too. As we recognize who and what shapes us, we see our impact differently. Consider the shaping and impacting you do every day in others' lives by how you lead, what you do, and whom you trust or don't trust.

To me, these borrowed words from author Ray Bradbury from his 1953 classic, *Fahrenheit 451*, offer perspective and pause: "Everyone must leave something behind when he dies, my grandfather said. A child or a book or a painting or a house or a wall built or a pair of shoes made. Or a garden planted. Something your hand touched some way so your soul has somewhere to go when you die, and when people look at that tree or that flower you planted, you're there. It doesn't matter what you do, he said, so long as you change something from the way it was before you touched it into something that's like you after you take your hands away. The difference between the man who just cuts lawns and a real gardener is in the touching, he said. The lawn-cutter might just as well not have been there at all; the gardener will be there a lifetime."[4]

What legacy are you leaving from your work? Where will people find you in what you've touched, molded, and shaped? Will your Trust, Inc. be the possibility seed inspiring others to create trust-cultures where people are engaged, innovative, and passionate about solving problems that plague our world? What will you leave behind?

Resources

Available at *www.nanrussell.com/trustinc.*

- ❖ **Discussion questions.** More insights and how-tos can evolve from discussing themes from the book in work groups, career book clubs, or professional development groups. Or you can use these discussion questions as personal development exercises.
- ❖ **Quick guides.** Short by-topic reference guides are available to download, including fundamental definitions, trust-building models, and key concepts.
- ❖ **Maneuver potholes.** Download a copy of "Seven Common Trust, Inc. Derailers, Potholes, and Mistakes"—questions and answers about common stumbling blocks and what to do about them on the path to your Trust, Inc.

- ❖ **Leadership tips.** Make trust more seeable, doable, and purposeful for your team with tips from a downloadable chapter, "Painting Pictures"—from *The Titleless Leader*.

- ❖ **Interactive blog.** Share your insights and challenges as a Trust, Inc. leader and find additional tips, resources, and commentary.

OTHER BOOKS BY NAN S. RUSSELL

The Titleless Leader:
How to Get Things Done When You're Not in Charge

Hitting Your Stride: Your Work, Your Way

Nibble Your Way to Success:
56 Winning Tips for Taking Charge of Your Career

For more information, go to *www.nanrussell.com.*

Notes

Unless otherwise cited, the quotations used in this book are from the author's collection. She started collecting motivational, inspirational, business, and insightful quotations in 1981.

PREFACE

1. "Jobless Recovery in the U.S. Leaving Trail of Recession-Weary Employees in Its Wake, According to New Study," TowersWatson.com, March 16, 2010, *www.towerswatson.com/en/Press/2010/03/Jobless-Recovery-in-the-US-Leaving-Trail-of-Recession-Weary-Employees-in-Its-Wake-According-to-New.*

INTRODUCTION

1. Andrew Kohut, "Americans Are More Skeptical of Washington Than Ever," *Wall Street Journal*, April 19, 2010, *http://online.wsj.com/article/SB10001424052702303 491304575187941408991442.html.*

2. John Wood and Paul Berg, "Rebuilding Trust in Banks," *Gallup Business Journal*, August 28, 2011, *http:// businessjournal.gallup.com/content/148049/rebuilding-trust-banks.aspx.*

3. "Americans Still Lack Trust in Company Management Post-Recession," Maritz.com, July 8, 2011, *www. maritz.com/Press-Releases/2011/Americans-Still-Lack-Trust-In-Company-Management-Post-Recession. aspx?from={F7761035-E6F1-43C4-847E-4549BDDA49A0}.* Content used with permission.

4. Michelle Goodman, "Lying on Your Resume: Why it Won't Work," ABCNews.com, June 24, 2010, *http:// abcnews.go.com/Business/resume-fibbers-lying-bio-work/ story?id=10994617.*

5. David Streitfeld, "The Best Reviews Money Can Buy," *The New York Times*, August 26, 2012.

6. Reed Abelson and Julie Creswell, "Hospital Chain Inquiry Cited Unnecessary Cardiac Work," NYTimes.com, August 6, 2012, *www.nytimes.com/2012/08/07/business/ hospital-chain-internal-reports-found-dubious-cardiac-work. html?ref=health.*

7. Nancy Kalish, "How Honest Are You?" *Reader's Digest*, January 2004.

8. Richard Pérez-Peña, "Harvard Students in Cheating Scandal Say Collaboration Was Accepted," NYTimes.com, August 31, 2012, *www.nytimes.com/2012/09/01/education/ students-of-harvard-cheating-scandal-say-group-work-was-accepted.html?_r=0.*

9. Andrew Hill, "Business Leaders Focus on Their Staff," *Financial Times*, January 9, 2013, *www.ft.com/intl/cms/s/0/21eea47a-58da-11e2-bd9e-00144feab49a.html#axzz2Njbbgjoe*.

10. "Trust in Government Suffers a Severe Breakdown Across the Globe," *2012 Edelman Trust Barometer* (January 23, 2012), http://www.scribd.com/doc/79027949/2012-Trust-Barometer-Press-Release

CHAPTER 1

1. Reinhard Bachmann and Akbar Zaheer, eds., *Handbook of Trust Research* (Northhampton, Mass.: Edward Elgar Publishing, Inc., 2006), 236.

2. Tom Clarke, "Students Prove Trust Begets Trust," Nature.com, March 13, 2003, *www.nature.com/news/2003/030313/full/news030310-8.html*.

3. Robert C. Solomon and Fernando Flores, *Building Trust in Business, Politics, Relationships and Life* (New York: Oxford University Press, 2001), 7.

4. Great Place to Work Institute, "About Us," GreatPlacetoWork.com, *www.greatplacetowork.com/about-us*.

5. Charles Feltman, *The Thin Book of Trust: An Essential Primer for Building Trust at Work* (Bend, Ore.: Thin Book Publishing Co., 2009), 7.

6. Tom Rath and Barry Conchie, *Strengths Based Leadership* (New York: Gallup Press, 2008), 2.

7. Sunada Takagi, "Thich Nhat Hanh: The most precious gift we can offer others is our presence," WildMind.org, March 27, 2007, *www.wildmind.org/blogs/quote-of-the-month/thich-nhat-hanh-most-precious-gift*. Used with permission.

CHAPTER 2

1. "Majority of American Workers Not Engaged in Their Jobs," Gallup.com, October 11, 2011, *www.gallup.com/poll/150383/majority-american-workers-not-engaged-jobs.aspx.*

2. Steve Tobak, "Why Employment Engagement Is Not Important (Yes, Really)," Inc.com, December 12, 2012, *www.inc.com/steve-tobak/employees-engagement-isnt-important.html.*

3. Tony Schwartz, "New Research: How Employee Engagement Hits the Bottom Line," HBR.com, November 8, 2012, *http://blogs.hbr.org/schwartz/2012/11/creating-sustainable-employee.html.*

4. Society for Human Resource Management, "Executive Summary: 2012 Employee Job Satisfaction and Engagement," SHRM Research Report, 2012.

5. Debra Nelson and Cary L. Cooper, *Positive Organizational Behavior: Accentuating the Positive at Work* (Thousand Oaks, Calif.: Sage Publications, 2007), 144.

6. Thomas Britt, "High Engagement and High Maintenance," *Business Execution Radio Podcast*, no. 57 (June 12, 2009), *http://blogs.successfactors.com/podcast/high-engagement-and-high-maintenance.*

7. "2012 Global Workforce Study: Engagement at Risk: Driving Strong Performance in a Volatile Global Environment," TowersWatson.com, July 2012, *www.towerswatson.com/en/Insights/IC-Types/Survey-Research-Results/2012/07/2012-Towers-Watson-Global-Workforce-Study.*

8. "Engaged Employees are Good, But Don't Count on Commitment," Clemson.edu, May 13, 2009, *www. clemson.edu/media-relations/archive/newsroom/articles/2009/ may/BrittEngagedWorkers.php5.*

9. Tom Rath, *Strengthsfinder 2.0* (New York: Gallup Press, 2007).

10. Jennifer Robison, "Wellbeing is Contagious (for Better or Worse)," *Gallup Business Journal,* November 27, 2012, *http://businessjournal.gallup.com/content/158732/wellbeing-contagious-better-worse.aspx.*

11. Gemma Robertson-Smith and Carl Markwick, *Employee Engagement: A Review of Current Thinking* (Brighton, UK: Institute for Employment Studies, 2009), 38.

12. William H. Macey and Benjamin Schneider, "The Meaning of Employee Engagement," *Industrial and Organizational Psychology* 1, no. 1 (2008): 22–23.

13. Daniel H. Pink, "The Puzzle of Motivation," TEDTalks.com, August 25, 2009, *www.youtube.com/ watch?v=rrkrvAUbU9Y.*

14. Teresa Amabile and Steven Kramer, *The Progress Principle: Using Small Wins to Ignite Joy, Engagement, and Creativity at Work* (New York: Perseus Books Group, 2011).

15. Daniel H. Pink, *Drive: The Surprising Truth About What Motivates Us* (New York: Riverhead, 2009). Kindle Edition.

16. Chris Hitch, PhD, "How to Build Trust in an Organization," UNC Kenan-Flagler Business School, UNC Executive Development, 2012, *www.kenan-flagler. unc.edu/executive-development/about/~/media/827B6E285F2 141C49D407DF7E5F5A1C4.ashx.*

17. Linda Myers, "What Is an Ounce of Integrity Worth in a Manager?" *Cornell Chronicle,* November 2, 2000, *http://news.cornell.edu/stories/2000/11/ hotel-managers-integrity-reap-higher-profits.*

CHAPTER 3

1. "Jobless Recovery in the U.S. Leaving Trail of Recession-Weary Employees in Its Wake, According to New Study," TowersWatson.com, March 16, 2010, *www.towerswatson.com/en/Press/2010/03/Jobless-Recovery-in-the-US-Leaving-Trail-of-Recession-Weary-Employees-in-Its-Wake-According-to-New*.

2. Tracy Mueller, "Missing Voices: Why Employees Are Afraid to Speak Up at Work," *Texas Magazine* (June 19, 2009), *http://blogs.mccombs.utexas.edu/magazine/2009/06/19/missing-voices-why-employees-are-afraid-to-speak-up-at-work*.

3. D. Harrison McKnight and Norman L. Chervany, *The Meanings of Trust* (Minneapolis: University of Minnesota Carlson School of Management, 1996), 33.

4. Ellen M. Whitener, Susan E. Brodt, M. Audrey Korsgaard, and John M. Werner, "Managers as Initiators of Trust: An Exchange Relationship Framework for Understanding Managerial Trustworthy Behavior," *The Academy of Management Review* 23 (July 1998), 516.

5. Jonathon D. Brown, "Understanding the Better than Average Effect: Motives (Still) Matter," *Personality and Social Psychology Bulletin* no. 28 (2012): 209.

6. "Self-Serving Bias," Wikipedia, *http://en.wikipedia.org/wiki/Self-serving_bias*.

7. "IA Releases Its 2011 Trust Survey Findings," InteractionAssociates.com, September 6, 2011) *www.interactionassociates.com/ia-releases-its-2011-trust-survey-findings*.

8. Edelman Berland, "Edelman Trust Barometer Finds a Crisis in Leadership," EdelmanBerland.com, 2013, *www.edelmanberland.com/press-releases/2013-edelman-trust-barometer-finds-a-crisis-in-leadership*.

9. "Americans Still Lack Trust in Company Management Post-Recession," Maritz.com, July 8, 2011, *www.maritz. com/Press-Releases/2011/Americans-Still-Lack-Trust-In-Company-Management-Post-Recession.aspx?sc_device=Maritz DotComPreviewContent.*

10. "New Metrics for a New Reality: Rethinking the Source of Resiliency, Innovation, and Growth" (LRN Whitepaper), *The How Report* (2012): 17.

11. Jeanne Sahadi, "You May Be Paid More (or Less) Than You Think," CNNMoney.com, March 29, 2006, *http://money. cnn.com/2006/03/29/commentary/everyday/sahadi/index.htm.*

12. Arie Nadler, Thomas Malloy, and Jeffrey D. Fisher, eds., *Social Psychology of Intergroup Reconciliation: From Violence to Peaceful Co-Existence* (New York: Oxford University Press, 2008), 3.

13. Ibid.

CHAPTER 4

1. Amy Lyman, *The Trustworthy Leader*, TrustworthyLeader. org, *www.trustworthyleader.org/eng/The_Trustworthy_Leader_Book.html.*

2. Sabrina Deutsch Salamon and Sandra L. Robinson, "Trust That Binds: The Impact of Collective Felt Trust on Organizational Performance," *Journal of Applied Psychology* 93, no. 3 (American Psychological Association, May 2008): 593–601.

3. Maria Williams, "Trusting Employees Supports Better Performance, Research Finds," WeKnowNext.com, August 31, 2011, *www.weknownext.com/workforce/ trusting-employees-supports-better-performance-research-finds.*

4. Liz Ryan, "Ten Signs You Work in a Fear-Based Workplace," *Bloomberg Businessweek*, July 9, 2010, *www.businessweek.com/managing/content/jul2010/ca2010078_954479.htm.*

5. Jack R. Gibb, *Trust: A New View of Personal and Organizational Development* (Los Angeles: The Guild of Tutors Press, 1978), 16.

6. Caleb Hannan, "Dish Network, the Meanest Company in America," Bloomberg Businessweek.com, January 2, 2013, *www.businessweek.com/printer/articles/89174-dish-network-the-meanest-company-in-america.*

7. Sean P. Mackinnon, Christian H. Jordan, and Anne E. Wilson, "Birds of a Feather Sit Together: Physical Similarity Predicts Seating Choice," *Personality & Social Psychology Bulletin* 37, no. 7 (July 2011): 879–892.

8. Sydney J. Harris Quotes, GoodReads.com, *www.goodreads.com/author/quotes/169034.Sydney_J_Harris.*

9. Robert C. Solomon and Fernando Flores, *Building Trust in Business, Politics, Relationships and Life* (New York: Oxford University Press, 2001), 118.

10. Nan S. Russell, *Hitting Your Stride: Your Work, Your Way* (Sterling, Va..: Capital Books, 2008), 162.

11. Cynthia L. Wall, *The Courage to Trust: A Guide to Building Deep and Lasting Relationships* (Oakland, Calif.: New Harbinger Publications, Inc., 2004), 140.

12. Scott Edinger, "Why Remote Workers Are More (Yes, More) Engaged," *Harvard Business Review* Blog, August 24, 2012, *http://blogs.hbr.org/cs/2012/08/are_you_taking_your_people_for.html.*

13. Erin Hong, "More Employers Believing Their Employees Will Work Regardless of Where They Are," DeseretNews.com, June 25, 2012, *www.deseretnews.com/article/865558072/More-employers-believing-their-employees-will-work-regardless-of-where-they-are.html?pg=all.*

14. Ellen M. Whitener, Susan E. Brodt, M. Audrey Korsgaard, and Jon M. Werner, "Managers as Initiators of Trust: An Exchange Relationship Framework for Understanding Managerial Trustworthy Behavior," *The Academy of Management Review* 23, no. 3 (July 1998): 517.

15. Daniel Kahneman, *Thinking Fast and Slow* (New York: Farrar, Straus and Giroux, 2011), Kindle Edition Location 1769-1771.

16. Rich Hanson, "How to Trick Your Brain for Happiness," *Greater Good Science Center Newsletter* (September, 2012). Used with permission.

17. Grabmeier, Jeff, "High Social Status Makes People More Trusting, Study Finds," *OSU Research News* (September 28, 2011), *http://researchnews.osu.edu/archive/statustrust.htm.*

18. Natalie Angier, "Why We're So Nice: We're Wired to Cooperate," *The New York Times*, July 23, 2002, *www. nytimes.com/2002/07/23/science/why-we-re-so-nice-we-re-wired-to-cooperate.html?pagewanted=all&src=pm.*

CHAPTER 5

1. Linda Galindo, *The 85% Solution: How Personal Accountability Guarantees Success—No Nonsense, No Excuses* (San Francisco: Jossey-Bass, 2009), book jacket.

2. Solomon and Flores, *Building Trust in Business, Politics, Relationships and Life,* 89.

3. David N. Goodman, "Saying 'Sorry' Pays Off for U.S. Doctors," NBCNews.com, July 20, 2009, *www. nbcnews.com/id/32011837/ns/health-health_care/t/ saying-sorry-pays-us-doctors.*

4. Linda Klebe Trevino and Michael E. Brown, "Ethical Leadership: A Developing Construct," in Debra L. Nelson and Cary L. Cooper, eds., *Positive Organizational Behavior* (Thousand Oaks, Calif.: Sage Publications, 2007), 101.

5. David P. Thompson, *Motivating Others: Creating the Conditions* (Princeton, N.J.: Eye on Education, 1996), 20.

6. Nan S. Russell, *The Titleless Leader: How to Get Things Done When You're Not in Charge* (Pompton Plains, N.J.: Career Press, 2012), 12.

7. Dov Seidman, "10 Practical Pointers for Capitalists from 10 Moral Philosophers," Forbes.com, January 31, 2013, *www.forbes.com/sites/dovseidman/2013/01/31/10-practical-pointers-for-capitalists-from-10-moral-philosophers/print*.

8. W. Chan Kim and Renee Mauborgne, "Fair Process: Managing in the Knowledge Economy," *HBR OnPoint*, 2003, *http://hbr.org/2003/01/fair-process-managing-in-the-knowledge-economy*.

9. Ibid.

10. Vilma Luoma-aho, Marita Vos, Raimo Lappalainen, Anna-Maiija Lamsa, Outi Usitalo, Petri Maaranen, and Aleksi Koski, "Added Value of Intangibles for Organizational Innovation," *Human Technology* 8, no.1 (May 2012): 13.

11. Faith Semercioz, Masoodul Hassan, and Zelal Aldemir, "An Empirical Study on the Role of Interpersonal and Institutional Trust in Organizational Innovativeness, *International Business Research* 4, no. 2 (April 2011): 128.

12. "New Metrics for a New Reality: Rethinking the Source of Resiliency, Innovation, and Growth" (LRN Whitepaper), *The How Report* (2012): 39.

13. Eric Patridge, *Origins: A Short Etymological Dictionary of Modern English*, 4th Edition, (London: Routledge, 1966), 740.

CHAPTER 6

1. "Theory X and Theory Y," Wikipedia, *http://en.wikipedia.org/wiki/Theory_X_and_Theory_Y*.

2. D. Harrison McKnight and Norman L. Chervany, "The Meaning of Trust," *Abstract* (1996), *http://citeseerx.ist.psu.edu/viewdoc/summary?doi=10.1.1.155.1213.*

3. Solomon & Flores, *Building Trust in Business, Politics, Relationships and Life*, 91–151.

4. Russell, *The Titleless Leader*, 28–31.

5. E.E.Cummings Quotes, GoodReads.com, *www.goodreads.com/quotes/7161-we-do-not-believe-in-ourselves-until-someone-reveals-that.*

CHAPTER 7

1. "Building Trust From the Inside Out: Engaging Employees as the New Influencers," *2012 Edelman Trust Barometer* (March 2012): 3, *www.scribd.com/doc/86070013/Building-Trust-from-the-Inside-Out-Engaging-Employees-as-the-New-Influencers.*

2. "2013 Executive Summary," *Edelman Trust Barometer* (February 2013): 5, *www.edelman.com/insights/intellectual-property/trust-2013.*

3. Elizabeth Wolfe Morrison and Frances J. Milliken, "Organizational Silence: A Barrier to Change and Development in a Pluralistic World," *Academy of Management Review* 25, no. 4 (2000): 721, 706–725.

4. Ibid., 710.

5. Mark C. Crowley, "Not a Happy Accident: How Google Deliberately Designs Workplace Satisfaction," FastCompany.com, March 21, 2013, *www.fastcompany.com/3007268/where-are-they-now/not-happy-accident-how-google-deliberately-designs-workplace-satisfaction.*

6. "What is Dialogue?," Clark University website, *www.clarku.edu/difficultdialogues/learn/index.cfm.*

7. "APA Survey Finds Feeling Valued at Work Linked to Well-Being and Performance," American Psychological Association Press Release, APA.org, March 9, 2012, *www.apa.org/news/press/releases/2012/03/well-being.aspx*.

8. Chuck Leddy, "The Power of Thanks," *Harvard Gazette* (March 19, 2013), *http://news.harvard.edu/gazette/story/2013/03/the-power-of-thanks*.

9. Peter F. Drucker, *The Essential Drucker: The Best of Sixty Years of Peter Drucker's Essential Writings on Management* (New York: Harper Business, 2001), 264.

10. Mathew Ingram, "The Kickstarter Principle: Crowdfunding Doesn't Work Without Transparency and Trust," GigaOM.com, March 29, 2013, *http://gigaom.com/2013/03/29/the-kickstarter-principle-crowdfunding-doesnt-work-without-transparency-and-trust*.

11. Kristine Hansen, "Bookstore Owner Turns a Page by Asking Customers to Spend More," Intuit Small Business Blog (March 28, 2013), *http://blog.intuit.com/marketing/bookstore-owner-turns-a-page-by-asking-customers-to-spend-more*.

12. "Transparency (behavior)," *Wikipedia*, https://en.wikipedia.org/wiki/Transparency_(behavior)

13. Brené Brown, *Daring Greatly: How the Courage to Be Vulnerable Transforms the Way We Live, Love, Parent, and Lead* (New York: Gotham Books, 2011), Kindle Edition, 44–45.

14. Secretary of State Hillary Rodham Clinton, "Remarks to the Press on Release of Purportedly Confidential Documents by Wikileaks," U.S. Department of State, State.gov, November 29, 2010, *www.state.gov/secretary/rm/2010/11/152078.htm*.

15. Brown, *Daring Greatly*, 16.

CHAPTER 8

1. Tony Simons, "Behavioral Integrity: The Perceived Alignment Between Managers' Words and Deeds as a Research Focus," *Organization Science* 13, no. 1 (Jan/Feb 2002): 20.

2. Tony Simons, Ray Friedman, Leigh Anne Liu, and Judi McLean Parks, "The Importance of Behavioral Integrity in a Multicultural Workplace," *Cornell Hospitality Report* 8, no. 17 (October 2008): 4. Used with permission.

3. Ibid., 15.

4. "Jobless Recovery in the U.S. Leaving Trail of Recession-Weary Employees in Its Wake, According to New Study," TowersWatson.com, March 16, 2010, *www.towerswatson. com/en/Press/2010/03/Jobless-Recovery-in-the-US-Leaving-Trail-of-Recession-Weary-Employees-in-Its-Wake-According-to-New*.

5. "Coal company executive withdraws from Stillwater takeover bid," *Daily Inter Lake, April 11, 2013*.

6. Jesse Davis, "Judge Makes Midnight Visit for Jailed Prosecutor," *Daily Inter Lake* May 1, 2013.

7. Phrases appearing in the chart were inspired by: Simons, *Organizational Science*, 18–35; Simons, *Cornell Hospitality Report*; "Integrity," *Stanford Encyclopedia of Philosophy*, open-source, September 2001, revision January 15, 2013, *http://plato.stanford.edu/entries/integrity/*; "Integrity," *The American Heritage Dictionary of the English Language*, 5th Ed. (New York: Houghton Mifflin Harcourt, 2011), 911.

8. "Integrity," *Stanford Encyclopedia of Philosophy.*

9. Brendan James, "Americans Say Obama's Ads Are More Honest, But Expect Both Sides to Lie," *Yahoo News* (September 26, 2012), *http://news.yahoo.com/esquire-yahoo-news-poll-romney-ads-lie-more-both-dishonest.html*.

10. Linda Myers, "What is an Ounce of Integrity Worth in a Manager?" *Cornell Chronicle*, November 2, 2000, *http://news.cornell.edu/stories/2000/11/hotel-managers-integrity-reap-higher-profits*.

11. *Daily Inter Lake*, "Montana School Official Apologizes for Plagiarism," February 10, 2013.

12. Lebaton Scharow, "2012 Ethics & Action Survey: Voices Carry," *Labaton Sucharow's 2nd Annual Integrity Survey of American Public* (September 2012), 1.

13. "Americans Still Lack Trust in Company Management Post-Recession," Maritz.com, July 8, 2011, *www.businesswire.com/news/home/20110711005277/en/Americans-Lack-Trust-Company-Management-Post-Recession*.

14. "Summary of Martiz Employee Engagement Poll 2012," Martiz Research Whitepaper, 2012, *www.maritzresearch.com/~/media/Files/MaritzResearch/Whitepapers/EmployeeEngagement_Summary_Review_2.pdf*.

15. Labaton Scharow, "2012 Ethics & Action Survey."

16. "Americans Still Lack Trust," Maritz.com.

CHAPTER 9

1. Russell, *The Titleless Leader*, 35.

2. "Authenticity," Wikipedia, *http://en.wikipedia.org/wiki/Authenticity_(philosophy)*.

3. Bruce J. Avolio, PhD, and Ketan H. Mhatre, PhD, "Advances in Theory and Research on Authentic Leadership," in Kim S. Cameron and Gretchen M. Spreitzer, eds., *Oxford Handbook of Positive Organizational Scholarship* (New York: Oxford University Press, 2012), 773–784.

4. Margaret Anne Meacham, *Life Stories of Authentic Leaders in Higher Education Administration* (Ann Arbor, Mich.: ProQuest, UMI Dissertations Publishing, 2007), 4.

5. Avolio and Mhatre, "Advances in Theory and Research," 783.

6. Ibid, 780.

7. "Brené Brown: How Vulnerability Holds the Key to Emotional Intimacy," *Spirituality & Health* (November– December 2012), *http://spiritualityhealth.com/articles/ bren%C3%A9-brown-how-vulnerability-holds-key- emotional-intimacy.*

8. Brené Brown, "4 (Totally Surprising) Life Lessons We all Need to Learn," Oprah.com (June 12, 2012), *www.oprah. com/spirit/Life-Lessons-We-All-Need-to-Learn-Brene-Brown.*

CHAPTER 10

1. Cadie Thompson, "Facebook: About 83 million Accounts Are Fake," USAToday.com, August 3, 2012, *http:// usatoday30.usatoday.com/tech/news/story/2012-08-03/ cnbc-facebook-fake-accounts/56759964/1.*

2. Solomon & Flores, *Building Trust in Business*, 4.

3. Laura Morgan Roberts, "Reflected Best Self-Engagement at Work: Positive Identity, Alignment, and the Pursuit of Vitality and Value Creation," in Susan David, Ilona Boniwell, and Amanda Conley Ayers, eds., *Oxford Handbook of Happiness* (Oxford, UK: Oxford University Press, 2012), 23.

4. Russell, *Hitting Your Stride*, 217.

5. Beth Pelkofsky phone conversation with author, May 7, 2013. Used with permission.

6. James R. Doty, MD, "The Science of Compassion," HuffingtonPost.com, The Blog, June 7, 2012, *www.huffingtonpost.com/james-r-doty-md/science-of- compassion_b_1578284.html.*

7. Mark C. Crowley, "Why You Need to Lead With Your Heart," FastCompany.com, October 15, 2012, *www.fastcompany.com/3002141/why-you-need-lead-your-heart?sf6630142=1.*

8. Adam Grant, "In the Company of Givers and Takers," *Harvard Business Review*, April 2013.

9. Transcript of conversation with Adam Grant and Knowledge@Wharton, "Givers vs. Takers: The Surprising Truth About Who Gets Ahead," DailyGood.com, April 24, 2013, *www.dailygood.org/story/419/givers-vs-takers-the-surprising-truth-about-who-gets-ahead-adam-grant-in-an-interview-with-knowledge-wharton/.*

10. Grant, "In the Company of Givers and Takers."

11. Jeff Greenfield, "Who Built It? We Did! The Democrats Rebut the GOP Convention," Yahoo.com, September 5, 2012, *http://news.yahoo.com/who-built-it--we-did--the-democrats-rebut-the-gop-convention-20120905.html.*

12. Roberts, *Oxford Handbook of Happiness*, 24.

13. Barbara Fredrickson, "The Science of Love, "AeonMagazine.com, March 15, 2013, *www.dailygood.org/more.php?n=5419.*

14. Ibid.

CHAPTER 11

1. Dennis S. Reina and Michelle L. Reina, "The HR Executive's Role in Rebuilding Trust," HREOnline.com, May 2, 2007, *www.hreonline.com/HRE/view/story.jhtml?id=12160414.*

2. "Promises, Lies and Apologies: Is it Possible to Restore Trust?"Knowledge@Wharton, July 26, 2006, *http://knowledge.wharton.upenn.edu/article.cfm?articleid=1532.*

3. Maurice E. Schweitzer, John C. Hershey, and Eric T. Bradlow, "Promises and Lies: Restoring Violated Trust," *Organizational Behavior and Human Decision Processes* 101, Issue 1 (2006): 1–19.

4. Maria Williams, "Trusting Employees Supports Better Performance, Research Finds," SHRM, WeKnowNext. com, August 31, 2011, *www.weknownext.com/workforce/ trusting-employees-supports-better-performance-research-finds*.

5. "Promises, Lies and Apologies," Knowledge@Wharton.

6. Michael P. Haselhuhn, Maurice E. Schweitzer, and Alison M. Wood, "How Implicit Beliefs Influence Trust Recovery," *APS Psychological Science Research Report* (2009).

7. Fernando Flores and Robert C. Solomon, "Creating Trust," *Business Ethics Quarterly* 8, Issue 2 (1998): 210.

8. Solomon and Flores, *Building Trust in Business, Politics, Relationships and Life*, 89.

9. Pamela Rutledge, PhD, "The Psychological Power of Storytelling," PsychologyToday.com, January 16, 2011, *www.psychologytoday.com/blog/positively-media/201101/ the-psychological-power-storytelling*.

10. Roderick M. Kramer, "Rethinking Trust," *Harvard Business Review* (June 2009), *http://hbr.org/2009/06/rethinking-trust/ ar/2*.

11. Ciara Torres-Spelliscy, "Trust But Verify...," The Hill's Congress Blog, March 1, 2011, *http://thehill.com/blogs/ congress-blog/politics/146813-trust-but-verify*.

CHAPTER 12

1. Bill Treasurer, interviewed by B.J. Gallagher, in "Courage Goes to Work," HuffingtonPost.com, March 29, 2012, *www.huffingtonpost.com/bj-gallagher/bill-treasurer-brings- cou_b_1380511.html*.

2. Mother Teresa Quotes, GoodReads.com, *www.goodreads. com/quotes/690241-i-was-once-asked-why-i-don-t-participate-in-anti-war*.

3. Prasad Kaipa and Navi Radjou, "Six Ways to Become a Wise Leader," DailyGood.com, April 2, 2013, *www. dailygood.org/story/411/six-ways-to-become-a-wise-leader-prasad-kaipa-and-navi-radjou-adapted-from-their-book/*. See *www.karmakitchen.org* for more information on and locations of the restaurant.

4. Ray Bradbury, *Fahrenheit 451* (New York: Simon & Schuster, 2003), 152.

INDEX

About the Author

Even a Stanford degree couldn't protect **Nan S. Russell** from being fired from her first professional job. Ultimately a good career move, it forced her to learn to thrive the hard way as she went from a minimum-wage employee to vice president of a multibillion-dollar company, spending 20 years in leadership roles, including as the architect and influence leader for a culture transformation for more than 10,000 employees.

Deciding to leave a successful career on the East Coast to pursue her lifelong dream to work and write from the mountains of Montana, today Nan has shared her workplace insights with a wide variety of people, from coal miners and Navy engineers to college students and senior leaders at Fortune 100 corporations and nonprofits, igniting passions, crystallizing thinking, and improving results.

Trust, Inc. is her fourth book. "Winning at Working," her work-insights column, appears in more than 90 publications, and she is a blogger for PsychologyToday.com on the topic "Trust: The New Workplace Currency."

Nan is an author, national speaker, and consultant, living with her husband, Dan, in the Rocky Mountains. She is pursuing her passion of helping individuals and organizations bring the best of who they are to the world.

If you'd like to connect with Nan, you can follow her on Twitter @nan_russell, friend her on Facebook at *www.facebook.com/nansrussell*, e-mail her at nan@nanrussell.com, comment on her blog or find out more about her and her work at *www.nanrussell.com*. She'd love to hear from you.